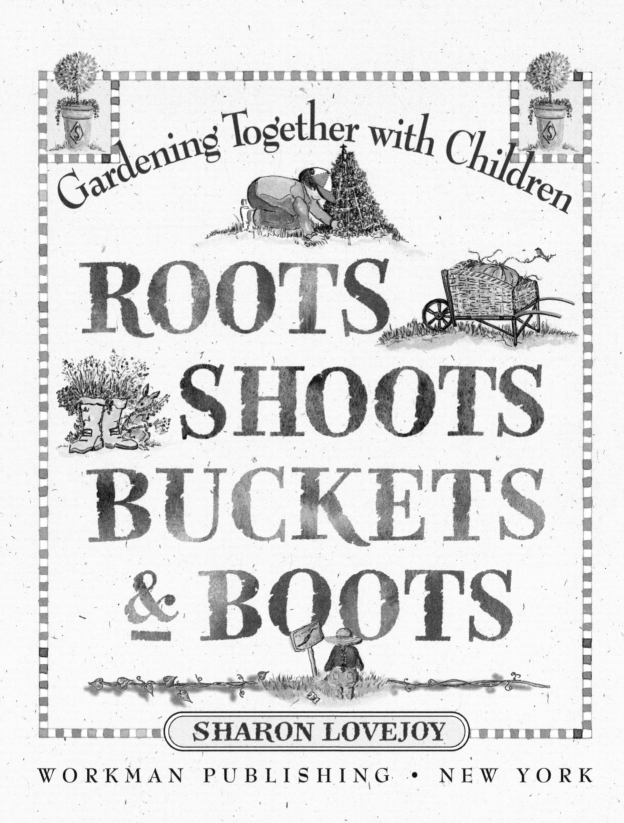

Gardening Together with Children

ROOTS
SHOOTS
BUCKETS
& BOOTS

SHARON LOVEJOY

WORKMAN PUBLISHING • NEW YORK

Library of Congress Cataloging-in-Publication Data

Lovejoy, Sharon, 1945—
      Roots, shoots, buckets & boots : gardening together with
children / written and illustrated by Sharon Lovejoy
            p. cm.
      Includes bibliographical references.
      ISBN 0-7611-1056-9
      1. Children's gardens.   I. Title   II. Title: Roots, shoots,
buckets, and boots.
SB457.L827 1999
635'.083—dc21   99-12457
                                                          CIP

Cover and book design by Lisa Hollander

Workman books are available at special discounts when purchased
in bulk for premiums and sales promotions as well as for fund-
raising or educational use. Special editions or book excerpts can
also be created to specification. For details, contact the Special
Sales Director at the address below.

Workman Publishing Company, Inc.
708 Broadway
New York, NY 10003-9555

Printed in the United States of America

First printing May 1999
10 9 8 7 6 5 4 3 2 1

Dedicated to
my husband Jeff and
my son Noah—
the two who taught me
to reach for the stars.

Acknowledgments

Without the tireless work of my husband and partner,
Jeffrey Prostovich, this book would never have been possible.

Special thanks to Ruth Sullivan, my intuitive editor who made this book what it is;
my fondest thanks to Peter Workman for believing in me;
Lisa Hollander for her creative design concepts;
Jamie Kennard for care with typesetting; copy editor Lori Eisenkraft;
and production manager Elizabeth Gaynor;
John Arnold and Patricia Berry for their inspiring Waffle Garden;
Jim Reynolds; Virginia and Max Holihan for providing us a warm Maine home;
Marta and Norman Morse for filling my reference shelves; Kate Stearns; Kris, Peter,
Lily, and Cole Christine; Sharon Christian Aderman; Agatha Youngblood;
Ellen Sheehy; Lea Yu; Skippy Shoemaker and Ginny Kirchenman;
entomologists Brian Harris and Louis Sorkin;
Dr. Steve "Buzz Man" Buchmann, author and scientist; Judith A. L'Heureux;
Vernon A. Quam; Rita Ebaakie, Zuni elder;
Holly, Alexa, and Bevan Shimizu and Jane Taylor for their Pizza Garden input;
Jeff and Liz Kellett of Windsong Herbs; and the Old Maine Art Shop.

A heartfelt thanks to Linda Ligon and my friends Fred Babb, Lance Evans, and
Janet Brownell; Pat Reppert for her pizza sauce recipe and friendship;
Susan Pendergast, Lynn Karlin, Marilyn Brewer, and Kary Gonyer;
all my friends and colleagues in the Cambria Writers' Workshop;
the fabulous editors at *Country Living Gardener* magazine;
and finally, to my dear friend Carol Stephens Yeates who handed me
my first Workman book in 1981 and said,
"You should do a book for them." It was worth the wait!

Preface

My life's work is deeply rooted in the soil of two sunny California gardens. The first, the garden of my childhood, is where I shared the world of nature with my grandmother. She knew that the surest way to destroy the enthusiasm of a young gardener was to dictate a steady regimen of rules and routine. Instead, we greeted each day as an adventure and learned to look for and expect miracles. The second, Heart's Ease, my community garden of the last decade, is a small, thriving plot of ground that attracts thousands of visitors annually. Both gardens, though separated by years and miles, nurture the same underlying theme: All knowledge is rooted in wonder, and what better place to cultivate wonder than in our own gardens?

When my son, Noah, was born, I started viewing the world of the garden through his thoughtful, cinnamon-brown eyes. He saw, sniffed, and heard things that had been lost to me somewhere between my childhood and growing up. As we gardened together I taught him how to separate crowded root balls and plant cuttings of scented geraniums. He taught me to listen to the crackling, firelike voices of the cottonwoods, to look at the kitty faces in Johnny-jump-ups, and to smell the faint scent of vanilla in the white heliotrope.

We both learned that the only rule we could count on in our daily garden experiences was that there are no rules; the only thing we could predict about Mother Nature is that she is unpredictable. So, every adventurous, unpredictable day in the garden was exciting and crowded with a kaleidoscope of sensory pleasures and the forgotten childhood miracles we found in unexpected places.

A decade ago my family's herb business moved into a tiny, tumble-down cottage and barn on a quarter of an acre of land in the heart of the village of Cambria-Pines-By-The-Sea. My dream for our new land was to re-create the old-fashioned gardens of my childhood and share the magic with townsfolk, tourists, and the myriad critters flying or ambling over our scrap of earth. I saw the promise of the soil and envisioned a tapestry of leaves and flowers; my husband and son had visions of wheelbarrow loads of soil and manure and the backbreaking reloca-tion of tons of rocks.

I knew from experi-ence the frustration of visiting perfect gardens of grandiose proportions and design. I wanted a garden composed of lots of ideas that would easily translate to small garden spaces, bal-conies, window boxes, or cramped, suburban yards. I wanted do-able, earth-friendly habitats that would inspire visitors to try it for themselves at home, wherever they might live. What I wanted most was a garden where grown-ups would include their children, because gardening together is one way to get back in touch with the earth and one another.

The Heart's Ease garden is now nearly fourteen years old. Through the years it has grown to cover every inch of available land, wall, and trellis with its unexpected beauty. It has spilled over the fences with an exuberance of green-ery that has spurred us to develop two new "idea" areas—a garden totally devoted to projects for children and a native habitat garden that effectively demonstrates our earth-friendly practices.

Our gardens have become inextri-cably bound to the lives of thousands of visitors and a loyal group of locals who use them as both a picnic area and a learning center. School groups meet for art classes and nature classes, the 4-H girls learn about beneficial insects and propagation, and geriatric groups gather for garden walks. Every November we host a Rosemary Festival and in April we have a Faerie Festival replete with singing trees and scarecrows dressed like faeries. The gardens have sheltered families holding memorial services for loved ones and young couples sealing their marriage vows. A recent letter of appreciation said, "I wanted to thank you for the respite and peace absorbed from just sitting in your gardens many, many times during several years of stress. I've used the bench at the rear as a place to regain some stability in the midst of beauty. Without knowing it, you have given me an important gift."

As the gardens spread and flourished, my son grew up and turned from flowers to football. Forgetting my own straying from the path at that age, I gave up hope and considered him one of the lost souls separated from the important simple pleasures and gifts of the earth.

One afternoon, after Noah had left home to attend college in a small city south of Cambria, he called and asked me to drop by for a visit. When I arrived, he whisked me out the back door to a yard that hadn't seen the blades of a mower in months. I grimaced and quietly followed him to a flat, sunny area where a dark rectangle of soil was shining through the unruly grass. We bent over the patch and Noah pointed to some tiny shoots just poking through the crust of earth. "Look, Mom, I planted a moonlight garden. It will be full of sweet-smelling white plants that will glow in the darkness and attract sphinx moths like the big ones we used to watch at night."

My eyes fogged under my dark glasses. I know I grinned like a fool as we discussed the promise of the newly dug earth, and I marked my mental scorecard with a "V" for victory for Mother Earth.

This book is my invitation to you to celebrate the earth with a child, to take the time to garden together, and to take journeys in your own backyard. Remember always that your child's knowledge will spring from the roots you planted deeply in the fertile soil of wonder.

Sharon Lovejoy

Contents

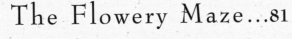

Introduction

"A child's world is fresh and
new and beautiful,
full of wonder and excitement."

—RACHEL CARSON, *A SENSE OF WONDER*

Twenty years ago on a sizzling hot day, I watched a grown-up teach a small group of children about gardening. The kids fidgeted and looked longingly toward the playground. They barely heard the teacher's instructions as he said, "Dig a square of soil, mark some straight rows with string, drop each seed into a hole, cover, water, and move on to the next row." I wanted to dive into the midst of the kids and share with them the countless miracles that could be found in a garden. And how every seed held the promise of flowers and fruits and all their attendant critters. I vowed then to someday write and illustrate a book that not only instructed, but also opened the eyes of both grown-ups and children to the many wonders in their own backyard.

I invite you to sit down with your children and get acquainted with my book. Turn to the Gardening Basics chapter (page 133), which is written for the novice as well as the seasoned gardner, where you'll find easy-to-follow instructions about planning, planting, and caring for your garden. My explanations about soil pH and other frequently asked questions are simply worded so that your youngster will understand the how AND the why of earth-friendly garden practices. Special projects in the Basics include making homemade seed tapes, building a simple wire com-

post bin, and constructing a cozy home for your own family of red earthworms. One of my favorite projects is assembling an Explorer's Kit (page 137) and using it every day and night in the garden. This assortment of inexpensive equipment adds another exciting dimension to your garden adventures.

The heart of this book is a collection of interactive "idea," or theme, gardens designed and tested for the inspiration and joy of children everywhere. Most plants in these gardens are easy-to-grow annuals which are suitable for most zones in the United States. They can be planted in June and enjoyed througout the summer and early fall.

Rather than focusing on a grown-up's concept of design, the gardens here are combinations of plants specifically chosen to captivate kids and engage all five of their senses. The nucleus of each theme garden is a "Discovery Walk," a daily (or nightly) exploration of nature in your own backyard.

At the end of each chapter are suggestions for recipes, craft projects, and activities to make with your harvest.

The Pizza Patch, Snacking & Sipping Garden, Mother Nature's Medicine Chest, and Zuni Waffle Garden introduce children to the incomparable taste of homegrown foods and drinks. Although these gardens are filled with edible plants, *not all parts of every plant are edible.* For example, while potatoes and tomatoes are edible, their stems, flowers, and leaves are *poisonous.* Teach your kids never to sample anything in their gardens until they check with you.

The Sunflower House, Moon Garden, Flowery Maze, and Garden of Giants each provide a "living" hideaway, a private place every child needs. Instead of the confining walls of a traditional playhouse, kids are surrounded by myriad vines and flowers and all the fascinating creatures they attract. Within their enchanted havens, they can read, play, create art, daydream, and just enjoy being alone. These natural shelters allow kids to grow along with their garden.

If you don't have enough space for one of the theme gardens described here, simply tailor it to fit your needs. My garden designs aren't set in concrete; they're grown in soil, so experiment, change, add to or subtract from them. Just follow the directions for planting and care requirements and your garden will thrive.

Browse through the first chapter on Top 20 Plants for Kids that I compiled from more than two decades of observations and teaching. Kids will learn to look at plants in a different way. If you don't have space for a theme garden, let your children choose one or more of the top 20 plants for a design of their own.

For planting in small spaces, read Buckets, Boxes & Boots (page 39) and you'll find there is always a place for a garden.

The Resources (page 153) provide invaluable aids for gardeners. Choose some catalogs listed in this section that look interesting to you and your kids. Contact the companies to request their most recent publication, and ask that it be mailed to your children. Kids love to receive mail, and this will build anticipation and excitement. When the catalogs arrive, set aside some dream time for yourselves, circle any plants that intrigue your youngsters, let them cut out photographs and paste them into their journals, and make plans for the magical garden you will create together.

Since children will be touching all and eating some of the plants, gardens should *never* be treated with herbicides, fungicides, or pesticides. Also, avoid the use of slug and snail bait, which can harm both kids and wildlife. In many cases, handpicking insects or a forceful spray of water (kids love to do both of these tasks) is all that is required to keep your garden pest free.

Children can discover the world in the microcosm of a garden, but they need to be accompanied on their explorations by a patient and enthusiastic grown-up, an earth-mentor who will enjoy the entire process of learning, planning, and gardening together.

The eloquent author and scientist Rachel Carson wrote, "If I had influence with the good fairy who is supposed to preside over the christening of all children I should ask that her gift to each child in the world be a sense of wonder so indestructable that it would last throughout life. . . . If a child is to keep alive his inborn sense of wonder without any such gift from the fairies, he needs the companionship of at least one adult who can share it, rediscovering with him the joy, excitement and mystery of the world we live in." It is my hope that YOU are that one special person. I wish you an exciting journey!

TOP 20
PLANTS FOR KIDS

When grown-ups ask me what they should plant for their children, my first inclination is to say "everything." The truth, however, is that just a few star performers in the plant world are a must in a child's garden.

My list of stars is short: twenty old-fashioned favorites that are more than pretty faces. They have personality, fragrance, texture, and color—vibrant color. They grow quickly—something kids need in response to their work. And they're versatile; they can be used as jewelry, toys, clothes, musical instruments, and household utensils.

My Top 20 plants are proven winners in thousands of gardens and are all available through catalogs or nurseries.

Pumpkins win all the popularity contests. If I had to choose only one plant to introduce kids to the wonder of gardening, it would be pumpkins—all shapes, colors, and sizes of pumpkins. Mini pumpkins, like the white 'Boo' or the palm-size 'Munchkin' and 'Jack-Be-Littles', grow best in tubs or barrels. Giant pumpkins need room to roam and are so rambunctious that they've

been known to engulf whole back-yards. My favorite, the flame-red 'Rouge Vif' d' Etampes', looks like an overstuffed piece of furniture—the kids in my gardens refer to this one as Cinderella's footstool. 'Connecticut Field', also known as 'Yankee Cow', is a descendant of a pumpkin Native Americans shared with the Pilgrims.

White 'Lumina' looks like a full summer moon shining through a tangle of prickly leaves. Carved, it makes a great jack-o'-lantern for Halloween, uncarved, it's a perfect white canvas for youngsters to paint with acrylics.

unflowers are the whimsical floral personalities in a child's garden. 'Giant Gray Stripe', 'Paul Bunyan', and 'Russian Mammoth' form towering, protective walls around playhouses, castles, tents, and meander-ing mazes. Diminutive 'Teddy Bear',

'Music Box', 'Elf', and 'Sunspot' are kid-size (2 to 4 feet tall) and can be grown successfully in containers. The bronze and golden 'Sundance Kid' will never grow up—it reaches only 18 inches at maturity, which makes it the perfect choice for a child's miniature fort or doll house planted in a shallow, wooden box.

Gourds are Mother Nature's all-purpose plants. From birdhouses to bath sponges, drums to dolls, a garden draped in gourds can supply children with endless hours of fun and discoveries.

Small, ornamental mixed gourds are perfect hideout plants and will quickly engulf a playhouse or tepee with vines and a blaze of papery, star-shaped blossoms.

One packet of seeds will produce colorful oddities that look like apples, pears, oranges, warty monsters, and strange crowns studded with thorns. Children "treasure hunt" for the ugliest, strangest, scariest, and prettiest offspring. Luffa gourds (or vegetable sponges) are shaped like giant cucumbers, and they have as many names as they have uses. Sepium, grown best in a half-barrel, is a small luffa that fits perfectly in a child's hand.

Plant a plot of bottle gourds and dipper gourds for a supply of winter craft projects. Tiny spoon gourds are child-size eating utensils and giant bushel gourds make perfect toy baskets. Two gourd cups connected by a long string can be used as a natural "telephone" and the long-handled gourds make great back-scratchers.

Corn is a source of wonder. Kids find it hard to believe that the needle-like seedlings that pierce the ground will someday produce exploding kernels or a whole harvest of jewel-toned ears.

Small corns, such as 'Strawberry' popcorn and mini Indian corn, are content to grow in close quarters, in half-barrels, and in baskets filled with rich soil and compost.

Giant 'Six-Shooter' corn can reach 12 to 15 feet. You'll need to set aside at least a 10-foot plot of sunny ground for this towering veggie. Or scratch out a maze design, and plant a maze of maize with your kids.

Berries attract kids as sure- ly as bugs attract toads. You can't go wrong if you start a patch, fence, or border of berries for your children. In my gardens the kids spend lots of time harvesting blackber- ries from the back wall. If they eat too many, they've learned that a fine stomach-settling tea can be brewed from the leaves.

Borders or pots of Alpine straw- berries are easy for kids to plant and grow. Each tiny, threadlike stem will take root and produce a com- pact, mounding plant dangling with ruby "earrings" of fruit.

Crushed berries pro- duce a "paint" that children can use in art projects or for face painting. In Sweden it's a tradition to string berries on grass or rush for

edible necklaces and bracelets. Kids poke the berries with a twig, thread them onto long, thin strands of grass, then tie with a knot. By the end of the day their jewelry has been nibbled away.

Hollyhocks, with their spires of colorful, silk-skirted flowers, belong in every child's garden. Line a fence with a planting of the perennial fig holly- hocks, old-fashioned singles, or 'Indian Springs', or etch a circle into the ground and plant a circular tepee as a hollyhock hideout.

These tall, graceful bloomers pro- vide kids with a summer-long supply of materials for an array of outdoor projects, and they furnish bumblebees, butterflies, skippers, and hummingbirds with a dependable source of sweet nectar. The rainbow-hued flowers are edible and kids enjoy stuffing them with cream cheese, ice cream, or sorbet.

Children can make puppets of flowers pierced with twigs and topped with unopened blossoms. Dolls are fashioned from fresh blossoms and unopened buds, stacked on top of each other and held together with twigs. Crowns, leis, and jewelry are crafted from the blooms strung on thread.

My favorite hollyhock story was told by Millie Baker Stanley of Ohio who, as a child, used to capture fireflies and tuck them into hollyhock blossoms. She then knit the edges together with a long twig and carried them through her moonlit garden like magical fairy lanterns.

arrots are the golden buried treasures in a child's garden. Pots, baskets, or window boxes filled with loose soil make a perfect carrot patch. Children love the small, round 'Thumbelina' and 'Parmex', and the baby-finger-size 'Minicors'. Kids can

arrange a "bouquet" of these tiny gems by tucking them, roots down, in a clear jar or vase.

Just for fun, mix some rocks and pebbles into a container of soil. When they encounter obstacles, carrots branch into whimsical shapes. Chances are good that the kids will unearth some very strange-looking carrot-people—much too interesting to eat.

imosa, or sensitive plant, has almost as many names as it has leaves—shrinking Susie, touch-me-not, humble plant, shame plant, sleepyhead, and ticklish Tim for its habit of rapidly folding downward when touched. This shy relative of the pea family is beloved by all children who are fascinated by a plant that moves quickly (fastest in hot weather and bright light) in response to their touch.

The *Mimosa pudica* is a small plant easily grown from seed. It is perfect for container gardening. Situate mimosa in an area where children frequently play or pass through so that they can constantly interact with their Mimosa plant.

Poppies are a brilliant, carefree addition to a child's garden. Sow the old-fashioned Shirley poppies with their tissue-paper skirts of pink, salmon, rose-red, and white. Enormous, saucer-size blooms of pink, orange, yellow, and apricot top the fuzzy wands of Iceland poppies. Go outdoors in the morning with your kids and watch this blowsy flower slowly burst the seams of its hairy, tight-fitting jacket.

Satin-petaled California poppies will lace your garden with silvery blue doilies of leaves. Their blazing flowers wear gray-green pointed wizards' caps. Watch them doff their caps before they bloom. These poppies are called little sleepyheads for their habit of closing up at the approach of night. Once kids become acquainted with this charming plant, they will seek it out to watch its evening ritual.

Wizard's Cap

Seed Pod

Poppies swaying on long, slender stems can be fashioned into dancing maidens. Gently fold back the silky petals and tie the "waistline" with a piece of grass. Leave the maidens attached to the growing plants. They'll look like a company of touring ballerinas.

Tomatoes are the main ingredient in a child's vegetable garden. Their favorites are the tiny golden currant, the yellow pear-shaped variety, the red cherry, and the marble-size green-grape tomatoes, which really do look more like grapes than tomatoes.

You can grow tomatoes in roomy containers in an area that's easily accessible. Kids will quickly get into the healthy habit of snacking on them whenever they pass.

My grandmother McKinstry shared stories of building "tomato-

people" with twigs and leaves. Simply pierce tomatoes with a twig, stack them to form a body, stick twigs through the sides for arms, and dress with leaves.

Trees are the spirits of a garden and the lungs of our earth.

Buy your child a "birthday tree" and plant it where it can be observed and enjoyed through every season. Take a yearly birthday photo to chart the growth of the child and the tree.

Plant hideout trees like weeping willows, Deodar cedar, black mulberry, and Camperdown elm. Kids will squeeze into the shady recesses and play happily for hours.

Harry Lauder's walking stick is a wildly twisted tree that is one of the most touched and loved things in a child's garden. This tree can be grown successfully in a container, and after a few years a child can cut walking sticks and crooked fishing poles.

Apple trees are laden with surprises. The delicate blooms are edible and make a great dessert topping on ice cream or pudding. Slice an apple horizontally and hold the slice up to a light. You'll discover the image of the blossoms you gathered in the spring.

Alliums are sometimes called "stinking lilies," because many members of this big family have a pungent aroma. These fail-proof plants will reward kids with a diversity of colorful, fascinating blooms that can be cut and added to bouquets or dried and used in craft projects.

Allium giganteum lives up to its

name by standing 4 feet tall and boasting show-stopping, 6-inch violet-blue flower heads. These starburst blossoms dry well on the stalk and make perfect scepters or wands. The dried hollow stems, pierced with holes, can be played like a flute or whistle.

Chives are some of the easiest plants for kids to divide and grow. Each tiny needle of green can be slipped into the soil. Chances are great that they'll root and multiply, and self-sow prolifically. Purple-flowered borders of chives are a magnet for butterflies, skippers, and bumblebees. The flowers are yummy fresh-picked and munched in the garden, or added to soups, salads, and sandwiches.

Potatoes are a vegetable most kids know and love. When hearing the word potato, most people think of the common brown spud found in every grocery store. But spuds come in a rainbow of colors—from gold to purple—and your own garden of potatoes can be

an exciting, colorful, scene of endless hunts for tasty, buried treasures.

Potatoes stuck with twigs make dogs, horses, elephants (with carrot noses), and even people. They can be carved into stamps for printing, and a Mr. Potato-Head can be made by decorating a spud with fruits and vegetables for the face. For hair, hollow out the top of the head, drop in wheat seeds, and water.

Woolly Lamb's Ear is an herb kids can't resist stroking and picking. They use the soft leaves as pretend moustaches, as blankets for fairy-size doll beds, and as clothing for tomato and flower dolls. When the weather is freezing cold in Holland, people sometimes lay a soft, velvety lamb's ear across their noses and under the bridge of their glasses for warmth.

Allium

Four-O'Clocks are exuberant, multicolored flowers with an old-fashioned dependability and punctuality. Go outdoors with your child any afternoon at 4:00 (with adjustment for daylight saving time) and watch the grand opening of dozens of blooms. Linger a bit and hummingbirds and sphinx moths may stop for a sip of nectar. Kids like to pick these flowers and slip them inside each other to form colorful chains of jewelry.

the green sepals like the fabric of a partially opened umbrella. Within a few seconds, the sepals open completely, the pistil protrudes, and the four petticoats of bloom unfurl.

To cheer a sick child confined indoors, cut a stalk of unopened buds and put them in a vase of water. At dusk turn out all lights in the vicinity of the plant and watch. The flowers will make a command performance—a special evening cotillion.

Evening Primroses, especially the fast-action 'Tina James' Magic, will provide your summer evenings with a magical explosion of blooms.

Establish a tradition of watching the slow, golden twilight dance of this primrose with your child. Just as the sun sets, the mature, pink-tinged buds begin to swell. Then the blooms quiver slightly and the pleated petals bulge out through

Radishes, from the Roman word *radix*, or root, are sometimes called "springers" because they sprout so quickly they seem to spring from the earth. Kids love the springers' prompt response to planting and can't wait to pull up the little roots and sample them.

Radishes come in a medley of colors and shapes. Easter egg varieties will give you a rainbow of red, white, lavender, and deep violet "eggs." Icicles surprise kids with their long, skinny white fingers. 'Saxa' can be harvested after only 18 days, and the German giant 'Parat' grows to the size of a baseball in less than a month. The giant of all radishes is the Daikon 'Moriguchi', which can reach a length of 5 feet—taller than many of the kids who can read this book.

Kids can slice daikon and use scissors or cookie cutters to make fanciful shapes for salad toppings. Radish animals are made with twigs or toothpicks—leave long hairy roots attached.

asturtium

flowers are so vibrant, they shine like jewels. Bite into a leaf or flower and you'll see why the plant earned its Latin name of 'nose-twister.' Use the peppery flowers, medallion-shaped leaves, or plump green pods to create a rainbow salad. Nasturtiums produce large seeds—easy for even the youngest child to plant. The seeds are virtually foolproof, germinating and putting on lots of growth (in warm, sunny areas) within weeks.

These vigorous climbers are content to grow in hanging pots and containers—I've even grown

them in old, worn-out work gloves nailed to a wall. The helmet-shaped blossoms make hats for flower dolls; or stuff them with cream cheese for a tart snack.

Moon Plant

was what my grandmother called this old-fashioned biennial, but you may know it as silver dollars, fairy pennies, gypsy jewels, penny flower, lunaria, Cinderellas, or elf platters. Moon plant self-sows prolifically and will grow well in problem shady areas—it tolerates neglect and even seems to thrive on it.

After the small pink flowers bloom, a flat green seedpod forms. Wait for the pod to turn brown, then show your child how to gently slip off the plain paper covering to expose the beautiful, iridescent Cinderella hidden inside.

Moon Plant

Children like to use the disks as play money, as hair and hat ornaments, or for fragile "porcelain" dishes. They can paint miniature scenes on the shiny rounds and hang them in fairy houses. Small clusters of the luminous pods, still on their branches, look beautiful tucked among the boughs of a Christmas tree.

When tiny, pink flowers drop their petals, the one-inch seedpod "moons" magically appear.

Lemon Verbena,

with its crinkly, lemon-tart leaves, is one of the most irresistible plants in any child's garden. Once you run your hands across the plant, you'll be hooked—lemon verbena lovers are for life.

Fresh new leaves make for great nibbling right in the garden. Gather the leaves and the tiny white flowers, shred them into small pieces, and use them as an ice-cream confetti. Put sprigs into pitchers of lemonade or iced tea to lend a sharp, zingy taste. Rub fresh leaves on your skin to discourage mosquitoes and other insects. Stuff a few handfuls of dried leaves into a pillowcase, and set it on a chair your child frequents—it will release a heavenly aroma.

Tie together two supple, young branches to make a perfect heart wreath, or fashion a crown for the kids with a circlet of branches.

THE PIZZA PATCH

PIZZA FOR BREAKFAST, PIZZA FOR LUNCH, FOR DINNER AND SNACKTIME, AND SATURDAY BRUNCH. TRY PIZZA AT MIDNIGHT, IT'S SURE TO APPEAL TO ANYONE YEARNING FOR THE WORLD'S PERFECT MEAL.

PIZZA TO GROW

The best pizza you'll ever taste is the one you make from ingredients grown in your own backyard. Your homegrown delight doesn't come from the typical straight-row vegetable garden you see in most yards. It sprouts and grows in a giant-size wheel that looks just like your favorite food. Imagine a six-foot-wide pizza cut into jumbo slices, outlined with a thick rock crust, and overflowing with your favorite toppings. That is exactly what you'll have when you plant a round pizza garden.

Gardening in the round is fun, easy, and never boring. Each slice of your pizza holds a new surprise, and every day in your garden reveals many magical changes. You'll nibble tiny, bite-size tomatoes, smell the powerful scents of herbal seasonings, and meet friendly, helpful garden critters. A harvest and a do-it-yourself pizza party are the grand finale to a summer spent out-doors tending a pizza big enough to satisfy a hungry giant.

Let the kids plan their own pizza garden. Include the toppings they like best, and add any or all of the ingredients listed at left.

Ingredients

3 seedlings, plum tomatoes

6 seedlings, cherry tomatoes

3 seedlings, small eggplants, such as 'Little Fingers'

3 seedlings, bell peppers

1 seedling, zucchini

1 seedling, rosemary

3 seedlings, oregano

3 seedlings, basil

3 seedlings, onions

3 seedlings, garlic

6 seedlings, 'Lemon Gem' marigolds

6 seedlings, 'Kablouna' Calendulas

Aged, bagged manure

Just for Fun

Grow one record-breaking 'Delicious' tomato plant. According to the GUINNESS BOOK OF WORLD RECORDS, this garden Goliath produced a 7-pound, 12-ounce tomato. One slice could cover the entire top of a pizza.

HOMEGROWN PLUM TOMATOES 15 ¢ EACH

SUNNYSIDE GARDEN

DROP MONEY INTO Honesty BOX

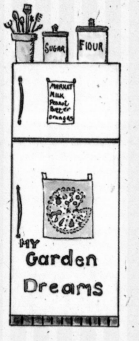

Plan Ahead

Draw a circle on construction or butcher paper and divide it into seven equal slices. Flip through garden catalogs and magazines for pictures of the plants in the ingredients list. Draw plants or cut pictures out of the catalogs, and paste them onto the slices.

PATHWAY

Place one of the five tall vegetables—plum tomatoes, cherry tomatoes, eggplants, bell peppers, and zucchini—in each of the five slices on the northern side of the pizza wheel. Cuddle the herbs, onions, and garlic together in one slice on the south side. Set aside one slice as a pathway. (It will look as if someone ate a piece!)

Bright golden marigolds and Calendulas are the color of cheese and make tasty toppings. Use them to fill in around the other vegetables and herbs.

Display the pizza plan on the refrigerator or a bulletin board, where you can see it every day. It will inspire everyone and build anticipation. You can use it as a "list" at the nursery and later as a map for placing your plants.

GOOD SOIL

Rainy Day Activity

Make plant markers for your Pizza Patch. Collect smooth, flat stones or buy wooden tongue depressors. If you are using stones, rinse and dry them before painting.

Choose a few colors of waterproof acrylic paint for decorating and labeling. Paint a picture of each plant and print its name on a marker.

Getting Ready

Select a flat 10-by-10-foot area that gets at least six hours of sun daily. Poke a stake into the center of the plot, and loosely tie the end of a 3-foot string to it. Have your child grab the end of the string, stretch it to full length, and walk in a circle. You can follow behind with a hoe and use it to outline the circular bed.

Prepare the bed for planting (see Preparing the Soil, page 140). Add a 2-inch layer of aged, bagged manure to the site, and work it well into the soil. Rake the plot smooth.

Outline the pizza with large rocks to form the thick crust. With a handful of flour, mark spots at 32-inch intervals along the crust. Drizzle flour from each of these points to the center stake. Mark these lines with smaller rocks. Remove the stake.

A Bite of History

The first pizza pies were flat rounds of oiled, herbed bread. The pizza we know didn't appear until Spanish explorers brought the tomato back from the Americas and adventurous Italian chefs added them to their pies. Presto! Pizza!

Planting & Care

Garden First Aid

Are your tomatoes, peppers, and eggplants flopping over? Use cut-up stockings to tie the plants to garden stakes. For instant support, surround the plants with tomato cages.

Begin planting when temperatures remain above 50°F. Stand in the center of your plot at noon on a sunny day. The shadow you cast will point north—that's where your tall plants will go.

To plant each slice, start from the center and work your way out, following your plan. The planting holes should be twice the width and depth of the seedlings' root balls (see Planting Seedlings, page 144).

Seedlings are fragile. Use a teaspoon to slip them out of their pots, and place them carefully into the holes. Add soil, pat it down, and water deeply, directing the spray at the base of the plants rather than the delicate stems and leaves.

Plants need their own share of soil, sunlight, water, and nutrients, so don't crowd them. Plant

tomatoes, eggplants, bell peppers, and zucchini 12 to 18 inches apart. The small
herbs will fit in one slice, but allow 6
inches between them, the onions, and
garlic. Scatter the "cheese" flowers
throughout each slice, leaving about 3
inches between them and other plants.

SPECIAL CARE

To control weeds and conserve moisture, lay a
2-inch layer of straw or shredded bark around
the seedlings. Do not cover their stems.

Poke your finger into the soil each day; if it feels
dry, water deeply. Feed your plants once a week with
a half-strength blend of liquid kelp and fish emulsion; after one month, give them a full-strength
feeding every four weeks.

Encourage tall, spindly plants to send out more
leaves by pinching off the tips at a node (the spot
where buds and leaves are forming). Deadhead
marigolds and Calendulas to keep them blooming.

Critter Control

Is something eating your young plants? Cut the bottoms out of paper cups, and slip one over each
seedling. Bury the bottom of the collar an inch deep in the
soil. The cups protect the plants as they grow. After a
month, slit the cups and remove them.

Sniff & Snoop

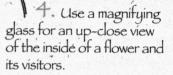

Visit your plants every day. Soon they'll become as familiar as old friends. Something magical and new is always happening in your garden. Take the time to discover it.

4. Use a magnifying glass for an up-close view of the inside of a flower and its visitors.

3. Put weeds and grass clippings in the compost. It's like money in the bank—or worms in your soil.

1. Shiny red ladybugs are your friends in the garden because they'll eat the pesky aphids.

Some females have wings

"**O**ne weed seeding equals seven years' weeding."

—OLD GARDEN SAYING

2. Fresh new leaves shine a brilliant green that attracts aphids. If you notice some on your plants, simply spray with water. Don't panic, and don't use poison.

5. Your "cheese" flowers, the Calendulas, will burst open like tiny golden suns. Pick a blossom, and taste its nutty flavor.

Tomato Bell Pepper Eggplant

6. A family portrait of members of the Solanacea family.

Silver slimy trails lead to slugs

Thugs and snails

8. Use a grapefruit rind as a lure to trap slugs. Dump them both into your compost or garbage.

Sit a Spell and smell the herbs

7. Taste the flowers and leaves of your herbs—they give pizza its flavor. Rub some rosemary needles onto your skin to chase off insects.

Basil Rosemary Oregano

Bumblebee Rumba

Watch a bumblebee zoom onto a yellow tomato blossom. Grasping the bloom tightly, she twirls and vibrates until the pollen explodes and dusts her hairy body. Then she grooms, pushing the pollen down into her tiny food basket, which she carries home to feed her colony.

The Pizza Party

Despite your snacking all summer, your Pizza Patch is bursting with delicious ripe produce. Tomatoes, eggplants, and peppers gleam like jewels, and zucchini seem to lurk under every leaf. It's time for harvest and a pizza party!

You're Invited

Spend time with your children cutting out and coloring pizza-shaped invitations for your party.

Harvesting the Crop

The day before the party, ask friends and neighbors to help gather and share the harvest. Provide baskets or buckets to fill with produce and herbs.

Once everyone gets going, they'll pick more than you could ever use at your party, so send them home with some of the bounty.

Ripe tomatoes should almost fall off the vine when their stems are lightly tugged and twisted. Show kids how to give tomatoes a tug test. Harvest the golden zucchini flowers to use as a topping, and the vegetables to use as sauce ingredients and toppings.

Eggplants and bell peppers damage easily if pulled off their plants. Use clippers to cut their stems, then remove the vegetables leaving a short piece of stem attached. Pull onions and garlic from the ground without removing their tops.

Pick marigolds and Calendulas, and lay them facedown on a paper towel. Snip sprigs of rosemary, basil, and oregano.

Rinse your vegetables, flowers, and herbs, and pat them dry with paper towels. Spread the harvest across your kitchen table for easy access.

It's best to make the sauce

and prepare the dough for the crust the night before the party. (You'll find recipes for both on pages 151 and 152.)

Your kids can help with the slicing, dicing, coring, and chopping (with adult supervision, of course). As you prepare the vegetables for the sauce, slice extras of everything, except tomatoes, to use as pizza toppings

the next day. (Slice tomatoes right before using.) Store the other toppings in covered containers and refrigerate overnight.

Making Your Own Pie

Before the guests arrive, place the prepared garden toppings and a pound of grated mozzarella in bowls to form an assembly line. Set up a child-high work area for your young visitors.

Preheat the oven to 500°F.

The fun begins when all the kids arrive. Uncover the dough. Punch it down, and separate it into small balls—one for each child. Help kids flour their work surfaces lightly. Show them how to flatten the dough balls with the heel of their hand. Pizzas can be round, or any shape they wish. Don't fret over uneven edges or holes—simply pinch the dough together to repair.

Place each pie on an aluminum pie plate. To keep things moving smoothly, one adult can brush the tops of the pizzas with olive oil and then spoon on the sauce. Let each child use the garden toppings to create a work of art that reflects his or her personality—a funny face, a portrait of a favorite pet, a fanciful landscape, or simply wild and colorful shapes.

An adult should place the pizzas in the oven. When the crust is golden brown (15 to 20 minutes), remove the pies from the oven, slide them onto a cutting board, and let them cool slightly before slicing.

Take photos of the kids each with their own pizza—then dig in!

SUNFLOWER

ALL SUMMER LONG, WE HID AND PLAYED IN THE SUNFLOWER HOUSE'S DAPPLED SHADE. AND CLOSE BESIDE US, RUSTLING LEAVES HAD CONVERSATIONS WITH THE BREEZE. A ROOF OF MORNING GLORY VINES TWISTED, TANGLED, INTERTWINED

HOUSE

Y ou can design and grow your dream house with just a handful of sunflower and morning glory seeds, some sunny ground, and water. Shaggy green walls topped with gold and russet flowers will enclose the perfect playhouse for tea parties, picnics, or quiet moments together. The slender tendrils of morning glories will twine their way up the sunflower stalks and form a lacy roof. The best days will be when you lie inside your house and look up at the heavenly blue morning glory sky and giant sunflower faces smiling down on you.

Ingredients

- 1 seed packet, 12-foot 'Russian Mammoth' sunflowers

- 1 seed packet, 5- to 8-foot 'Valentine', 'Velvet Queen', or 'Evening Sun' sunflowers

- 1 seed packet, 1- to 2-foot 'Elf', 'Music Box Mix', or 'Sundance Kid' sunflowers

- 1 seed packet, 'Heavenly Blue' morning glories

EQUIPMENT:

- 1 40-pound bag aged manure

- 3 bags shredded bark or straw

- 1 roll of twine

Your Sunflower House will attract all kinds of visitors. Hummingbirds will zip in for a sip of nectar, and ladybugs will feast on pollen. Orange-and-black painted lady butterflies will land and deposit their eggs on the foliage.

Lady Luck

If a ladybug lands on you, close your eyes and make a wish.

Getting Ready

Select a flat 10-by-10-foot area that gets at least six hours of sun daily and is sheltered from wind. Stand in the center of your plot at noon; the shadow you cast will point north. Using a stick, trace out a 6-by-9-foot rectangle in the ground; one of the shorter sides should face directly north.

String roof twined
with morning glories

Tall, medium,
and short
sunflowers

Following the outline, dig a narrow, 6-inch-deep
planting trench. Prepare the trench for planting (see
Preparing the Soil, page 140). Add well-aged manure
or compost to the soil and fill in the trench. Cover
the entire 10-by-10-foot rectangle, except for the
planting area, with a 3-inch layer of shredded bark or
straw. This mulch will deter weed growth and provide
a soft play area. The night before planting day, place
the morning glory seeds in lukewarm water. By morning, their tough coats will soften so they will sprout.

Pod
Furniture

Mother Nature provides everything you need to furnish your Sunflower playhouse. Make dishes and utensils from lunaria disks, acorn caps, walnut shells, and love-in-a-mist, eucalyptus, and milkweed pods. A stump is a perfect table; use shorter stumps for stools.

Planting & Care

Begin planting when temperatures remain above 50°F. To mark the spots where you'll plant seeds, drop small handfuls of flour 4 feet apart in the trench. Leave a 2-foot gap for the doorway on one of the short sides. Poke two 1-inch holes into the middle of each spot of flour. Drop a 'Russian Mammoth' sunflower seed into one of the holes; pop a morning glory seed into the other. Plant the rest of the sunflower seeds (the small and medium height) at 4-inch intervals between the big ones (see Planting Seeds, page 141).

SPECIAL CARE

Newly sown seeds need to be kept moist to germinate. Water your garden daily with a gentle spray from a watering can. Feed your plants every two weeks with a half-strength blend of liquid kelp and fish emulsion. When your plants are about 4 inches high, give them a full-strength feeding every four weeks, and water when necessary (do the poke test with your finger to see if soil is dry).

Cutworms and slugs will have their eyes on the emerging giant sunflowers. To protect the delicate shoots, cut the bottom out of a paper cup and slip it over each plant and its morning glory neighbor. When the sunflowers are about 6 inches high, slit the cup and slip it off.

If necessary, sink sturdy stakes at least 12 inches into the soil to support the biggest sunflowers. Dead-head the small sunflowers, pinching or snipping at the node just below the worn-out blossom.

When the morning glories reach the top of the sun-flower stalks, loosely tie a 7-foot-length of twine just below the head of the tallest sunflowers. Carry the lengths of twine across the rectangle and tie them care-fully under the heads of the giant plants on the opposite side. The morning glories will creep across the twine to form the roof of your Sunflower House.

April Flowers

The Hidatsa tribe called April "mapi'-o'ce-mi'di," or the Sunflower-planting Moon. Sunflowers were the first crop planted in the spring and the last crop harvested in the fall.

Secret Hideaway

Your Sunflower House is your private hideaway through the dappled days of summer. Stock it with your favorite books and toys and keep your Explorer's Kit nearby.

3. Use a magnifying glass to inspect a sunflower head. It consists of rays and disks. Like welcome banners, the rays entice insects to feed on and pollinate the disks.

2. Measure a stalk of the 'Russian mammoth' sunflower every week and record the number of inches it grows.

1. Their name is morning glory for a reason. Catch them opening their bright blue eyes about 5 A.M.

Blest Be the Sunny Hours

Sunflower Towers

AUGUST
JULY
JUNE
MAY
APRIL

4. As your house grows, take turns standing inside, next to a sunflower, and photographing each other.

Moist sand for Butterflies

5. Do morning glory tendrils always twine in the same direction?

6. Sunflower leaves make delicious salads for hungry birds.

7. Cut lots of bouquets. More flowers will grow as you pick.

8. Go on a bug safari. Have you noticed foam on the sunflower leaves? This "frog spit" is where the froghopper nymph hides. Look closely at the bubbles and if you're lucky, you'll see the nymph's tail pumping lather from its abdomen.

Within a few days of planting, a sunflower seed splits open and a thin root threads its way through the soil in search of moisture. Soon a green stem peeks from the shell and grows upward until it breaks through the crust of the earth.

Harvest Treats for the Birds & Bees

As autumn days shorten, frosts wither the leaves and vines of your Sunflower House. The tightly packed seeds begin to ripen, and forty-three species of birds, such as cardinals, jays, and goldfinches, help themselves to the feast. When the backs of the flower heads turn golden brown, it's time to cut and dry them. Pick a supply of seeds to nibble while you dream of next summer's Sunflower House. Invite friends to share your harvest and do the following projects.

Stalk Hotel

Some of the most active pollinators in the garden are peaceful dwarf carpenter bees, mason bees, and leaf cutters, which like to make their homes in the pithy stems of sunflowers. To make sure they

have warm winter lodgings, nail a clean one-pound coffee can to a mounting board and stuff it with stalks. Attach the board to a sheltered spot on your house or an outbuilding.

Harvest Wreath

Lay freshly harvested giant sunflower heads faceup on a work surface. Cut and remove the center of the sunflower head. The remaining ring is the base for an autumn wreath. Using glue, attach a cluster of acorns, pods, nuts, or cones to the top of the ring. Let the wreath dry completely. Tie a length of raffia or ribbon around the top and hang.

Sunflower Garlands

In Nordic countries, people believe that sharing the crop with the birds on Christmas Eve ensures a bountiful crop and a year of good weather. To make a sunflower garland, poke a hole through the top of a dried sunflower head and string a wire through it. Using the wire, attach the flower head to a rope strung between trees or fence posts. Keep adding heads until the rope is full.

Sunflower Treats

Preheat the oven to 200°F. Shake or pick out the ripe seeds from dried sunflower heads. Spread the seeds on an ungreased cookie sheet, and salt them lightly. Bake for 3 hours, stirring once each hour.

Remove from the oven, and let cool. Pour the seeds into a covered container and store in a cool place. Whenever you're hungry or tired, snack on your sunflower seeds for a high-protein energy boost.

Save some of your browned sunflower seeds and spread them on a work surface covered with a 12-inch sheet of waxed paper. Use a rolling pin or potato masher to crush the seeds into a coarse meal.

Pour the meal into a bowl, add 1 tablespoon of peanut butter, and mix together with a fork. Add more peanut butter until the mixture is firm. Roll into Ping-Pong-size balls.

Native Americans of the Hidatsa tribe depended on sunflowers for a plentiful supply of high-protein energy snacks. After harvesting and drying, they parched the hulled seeds in a clay pot and ground them with a pestle or rock. Then they rolled the oily, ground meal into small balls that they carried in a skin pouch and nibbled when hungry.

Wrap in waxed paper or plastic wrap and store in the refrigerator for snacking.

Be sure not to bake all the seeds so you can send your friends home with some, along with directions for growing their own Sunflower Houses next spring.

Container Gardens

BUCKETS BOXES & BOOTS

YOU DON'T NEED LAND OR EVEN A POT

THE SECRET TO GARDENING IS... ...USE WHAT YOU'VE GOT

Even if you live in a houseboat or a city apartment, you can grow an amazing garden. You don't need land, or very much space, but you do need a sense of humor, a good imagination, light, soil, water, a collection of containers, and plants.

Once you're hooked on gardening in containers, you will look at things differently. Common castoffs and whimsical objects tantalize you into designing a medley of unusual, easy-to-care-for gardens. Wouldn't the rusty old colander in the kitchen cupboard provide great drainage for a cactus collection? Could the broken laundry basket you stuck in the closet be the right size and depth for a cut-and-come-again salad garden? You won't know until you dig in and   get growing.

LITTLE GREENTHUMBS
South Bristol, Maine

TUB O' SPUDS

All spuds aren't created equal. There are hundreds of varieties to choose from and they come in a rainbow of colors—from red and gold to blue and purple. You and your gardening pals will be spoiled forever when you taste your first harvest of these homegrown buried treasures.

Ingredients

1 pound seed potatóes:
   Ruby crescent
   Yellow fingerling
   Yukon gold
   Blue
(choose one or mix)

EQUIPMENT:

1 half-barrel or galvanized tin
   tub, 20", wide x 18"deep

nylon screening

bagged potting soil

bagged, aged manure

Getting Ready

To sprout the seed potatoes, put them in a brown paper bag with a whole banana or apple. Roll down the top of the

Make It Your Own

Search cupboards, closets, and the attic for objects that can become eye-catching planters. Visit nurseries and public gardens and page through catalogs for plant ideas for a pocket-size garden.

Even the smallest container gardens are irresistible.

bag to seal it, and place it in a warm spot. A week later, sneak a peek. The spuds should have short sprouts popping from their growth buds, or eyes. If they haven't sprouted, wait a few days and check again. Cut the potatoes into small pieces with two or three sprouted eyes in each.

Drill four ½-inch drainage holes in the bottom of the container, and cover the openings with pieces of nylon window screening. See Container Gardening, page 144. If you're using a barrel that's old and full of holes, lay a piece of screen across the bottom.

Set the container in a spot that gets at least six hours of sunshine daily—preferably cool, morning sun. Fill with potting soil to a depth of 6 inches. Mix in a shovelful of aged manure. Don't worry about the shallow soil depth. You'll be "hilling" soil and manure on top of your spuds throughout the season, so by harvest time your tub will be full.

Planting & Care

Begin planting your spuds when temperatures remain above 55°F. Set the sprouted chunks on the soil about 6 inches apart with the eyes to the sky. Cover them with an inch of potting soil, and water gently. This shallow covering will force them to make an early appearance.

Poke your fingers into the soil daily to make sure it is moist, but not soggy. Spuds will rot if kept too wet.

Within a few days, you'll see the first green vines. When they are 4 or 5 inches long, make a little hill over each with a mixture of soil and aged manure. Leave 2 inches of vine exposed. Repeat this process each time the vines reach about 5 inches.

Potatoes-Buried Treasures

Nibble of History

New World gardeners have grown the humble spud for more than ten thousand years. Until the 19th Century, Europeans grew the potato only for its decorative vines and flowers as they feared that the knobby tuber itself was poisonous. Today, spuds are the world's most popular vegetable.

Watch for the first starry blossoms to appear, and note the date on a calendar or in a notebook.

TATER TIME

About two weeks after the potato vines blossom (check your notebook for the date), you can have a harvest preview. Slip your fingers into the loose soil beneath a vine to feel for marble-size tubers. Gently twist a few off their stems. Cook and eat these tasty treats.

Later in the summer, your vines will signal the real harvest time, when they wither and die. Tip the tub on its side, pour out the contents, and spread the spuds on newspaper to dry. Toss the old soil into your compost pile, as you'll want to use clean, new soil for next year's crop. Store potatoes in a cool cellar or cupboard (about 45° to 50°F), but never refrigerate.

WINDOW BOX

Your dazzling window boxes deserve a place in the spotlight. Mount them in an area where you and the kids can enjoy them throughout the day.

The little garden suggested for a sunny window has color with a capital C. It's as bright as a box of crayons. The shade window garden is a rich tapestry of blues, purples, and pinks. Your neighbors will enjoy them, too.

Ingredients

FOR SUNNY BOXES:

6 seedlings, zinnias (tall)

4 seedlings, California poppies (medium)

6 seedlings, Portulacas (short)

6 seedlings, verbenas (trailing)

FOR SHADY BOXES:

6 seedlings, coralbells (tall)

4 seedlings, wishbone flowers (medium)

4 seedlings, forget-me-nots (short)

6 seedlings, Lobelias (trailing)

EQUIPMENT

1 wooden, plastic, or metal window box, at least 24 inches long by 8 inches wide by 6 inches deep

drill

mounting supports

nylon screening

potting soil

Getting Ready

Check the amount of direct sunlight received by your windows. For sun-loving flowers, choose a

window that gets four to six hours of sunlight daily;
shade plants thrive on cool north- and east-facing
walls. Mount the window box.

Planting & Care

Begin planting when temperatures remain above
70°F. Design the box just as you would a
flower garden planted in the ground: Place the tall
plants in the back, the medium-size ones in the middle,
the shortest ones in the front, and the trailing ones
along the edges.

Make certain there are at least three drainage holes in the box. Cover the openings with screening, then fill the box with bagged potting soil.

The planting holes should be twice the width and depth of the seedlings' root balls. Pretreat the holes with vitamin B_1 (see Planting Seedlings, page 144).

Moisten the seedlings. Use a teaspoon to gently remove them from their packs, and plant them 3 inches apart in staggered rows. Tuck the trailing plants along the front and side edges of the box so they cascade down the sides.

Window boxes are nearly carefree and almost impossible to neglect. How could you ignore the simple needs of a riotous box of flowers peering through your window? Boxes in the sun dry out rapidly, so check daily for moisture. Deadhead spent blooms. Two weeks after planting, begin feeding your plants once a month with a blend of liquid kelp and fish emulsion. (Be sure to moisten the soil with water before you fertilize.) And don't forget to cut plenty of colorful flowers for bouquets; the more you snip, the more they'll bloom.

Indoor Gardens

Indoor container gardens thrive near sunny windows if you provide them with water, fertilizer, and a constant temperature of 65° to 70°F—no cold drafts or blasts of heat. If plants need more lighting, buy a 48-inch fluorescent light and suspend it above the plants.

Window Seat

Watch your poppies shed their pointed green caps and slowly unfold their silky petals in the morning. At sunset, they'll close their petals for sleep. You aren't the only ones enjoying your window box. Butterflies will stop by for a sip at the zinnias and verbenas. Hummingbirds will dive into coralbells for a quick drink, and Lobelia attracts hover flies.

WATER GARDEN IN A BARREL

Water is the magical elixir that brings life to a garden. It beguiles kids, adults, and wildlife alike.

The plants in this barrel work together to oxygenate the water and keep each other healthy. Those that grow with their heads above water shade the surface and block the growth of algae; they also provide places for fish to hide. The dangling roots of

EQUIPMENT

1 wooden half-barrel, at least 28 inches wide and 17 inches deep

1 bottle liquid dechlorinator

1 20-pound bag fine gravel

ordinary garden soil

6 6-inch-wide plastic containers

fertilizer tablets

a few bricks

....

6 water snails

6 mosquito fish

Ingredients

FLOATERS:

1 water lettuce

1 water hyacinth

SUBMERGED PLANTS:

1 Vallisneria

1 Cabomba

OTHER PLANTS:

1 four-leaf clover

1 horsetail

1 dwarf papyrus

1 dwarf water lily, such as 'Ellisiana' or 'Hermine'

floaters absorb fish wastes. Submerged plants oxygenate the water.

Critters help out, too, keeping the water clean and mosquito free. The best choices are mosquito fish, which can often be obtained from your local cooperative extension service. Avoid goldfish, as they overload the water with wastes.

Getting Ready

Set the barrel in a spot that receives three to four hours of sun daily (preferably gentle morning light) and is away from overhanging branches that may drop leaves. Fill the container with water, and let it sit for a few days. At first the barrel may leak, but the wood will soon swell and hold the water. Drain, refill to within an inch of the rim, then add dechlorinator and the plants. Fish should be added about two weeks after planting.

Planting & Care

Begin planting when temperatures remain above 70°F. Floaters drift at the whim of the winds and need no anchor. The other plants must be potted if you did not buy them in containers. Gently insert the roots of the Vallisneria and Cabomba into gravel-filled pots, and set them on the bottom of the barrel.

For each of the other plants, put garden soil and a fertilizer tablet in the bottom half of a 6-inch-wide plastic container. Support the plant while adding soil to a depth of 1 inch below the rim. The crown (where the roots meet the stem) should be

Dwarf papyrus

Four-leaf clover on cement block

Submerged Vallisneria in gravel-filled pot

Water lily sits on the bottom of barrel

Block or brick to elevate horse-tails

Cleaning Crew

Snails are the cleaning crew, eating algae day and night. Gambusia, or mosquito fish, never need feeding because they're so busy gobbling mosquito larvae.

visible. Top with a 1-inch layer of fine gravel. Using bricks or blocks to adjust the level of the pots, place the four-leaf clover, horsetail, and dwarf papyrus so that the top of the pot is about 6 inches below the water's surface. Set the potted water lily on the bottom of the barrel.

After about two weeks, add the snails and fish. Fish and snails are sold in plastic bags filled with water. Before releasing, accustom them to the new water temperature by floating the closed bags in the barrel for fifteen minutes.

Keep the barrel filled with dechlorinated water, and pinch off yellowing leaves. If the container becomes overcrowded with floaters, compost them; *never* throw them into streams or lakes as they will choke out native plants. Don't worry about slight algae growths.

Splish Splash

Lift a water hyacinth. Can you see how fish could hide out in its petticoat of roots? Push your floaters underwater, and see what happens. Floaters have air-filled stems and leaves that act as tiny life preservers.

Water lilies are as dependable as clocks, opening and closing at the same time each day. While they're open, sniff their exotic fragrance.

Slide your fingers down the stems of horse-tails. Do you see why Native Americans used these plants to scour pots?

BOOT CROP

Worn-out boots make perfect containers for a garden that's a tiny version of the one Mr. McGregor grew. Plant a pair of miniature gardens, and be on the lookout for the visits of animal friends—maybe even hungry little Peter rabbits.

Ingredients

2 seedlings, parsley

2 seedlings, chamomile

1 seed packet, 'Easter Egg' radishes

1 seed packet, 'Thumbelina' or other mini carrot seeds

EQUIPMENT:

1 pair of boots

nylon screening

bagged potting soil

Planting & Care

Choose a spot for the boots that receives at least four to six hours of sunlight daily. Begin planting when temperatures remain above 65°F. Drill drainage holes in the boots, and cover the openings with screening. Fill the boots to the rim with soil, and tuck the parsley seedlings into the heel end. Plant the chamomile in front, and then rake the soil in the center of the opening with a fork. Sprinkle radish and carrot seeds over this area. Press the seeds into the soil with a spoon, and water the entire planting gently. See Planting Seeds, page 141, and Planting Seedlings, page 144.

Tending your boot garden takes about as much time as tying your shoes. Push your finger into the soil daily. Water if the soil feels dry. In less than a week, the radishes will poke

Hats off for this garden! Line an old hat with a plastic bag, fill with soil and you'll have a head-turning planter.

Kid Gloves

....

Fill a pair of worn work gloves with soil. Tack them onto a fence or post, and tuck an Alyssum into each. Press four or five nasturtium seeds into the surface of the soil, and water gently. Within days, you'll have a miniature garden that isn't a handful.

through the soil. The tiny, lacy leaves of the carrots will emerge next. Whenever you harvest a few vegetables, sprinkle more seeds in the boot to ensure a continuous crop.

Feed your plants every two weeks with a half-strength blend of liquid kelp and fish emulsion. (Moisten the soil before fertilizing.) Within three weeks, radishes will be ready for plucking. They taste great thinly sliced and layered on sandwiches.

Use parsley for salads, cheese dips, and soups. Snip off chamomile blossoms, which Peter Rabbit's mother used to make tea for the naughty bunny. Steep some for yourself, too.

SNACK AND SIP THE WHOLE DAY THROUGH.

ONE FOR ME AND TWO FOR YOU.

Sun Tea

SNACKING & SIPPING GARDEN

Sun-warmed treats and tasty teas are at your fingertips when you plant a Snacking and Sipping Garden. Here, four heart-shaped beds form a gigantic shamrock thickly planted with luscious vegetables, fruits, herbs, and edible flowers. Enjoy them right off the plant while you care for your garden, or use them in your favorite dishes.

Ingredients

INNER CIRCLE:

1 seedling, lovage

SHAMROCK:

1 seedling, 'Sun Gold' cherry tomato

1 seedling, 'Super Sweet 100' cherry tomato

1 seedling, tomatillo

1 seedling, lemon cucumber

1 seed packet, borage

1 seed packet, 'Early Sunglow' or 'Kandy Korn' corn

BORDERS:

4 seedlings, mint (spearmint, chocolate mint, or orange bergamot)

1 seed packet, radish

1 seed packet, nasturtiums

4 six-packs, Johnny-jump-up seedlings

1 six-pack, alpine strawberry seedlings

1 40-pound bag aged manure

Savor lemon yellow cucumbers and bite-size tomatoes. Nibble tiny corn ears and alpine strawberries small enough for fairies to eat. Sample spicy nasturtium leaves, flowers, and pods, and quench your thirst with zingy herb teas made in the sun and sipped through Mother Nature's straws.

A Star is Born

Fuzzy borage is spangled with starry blue flowers that attract busy pollinating insects. Surround cucumbers, tomatoes, and alpine strawberries with borage to ensure a bountiful crop.

Getting Ready

Select a flat 12-by-12-foot area that gets at least six hours of sun daily. Stand in the center of the plot, and use a hoe to make a circle 2 feet in diameter. Then, following the diagram below, outline four heart-shaped "leaves" to form a giant shamrock. Each leaf should be about 4 feet across at the widest

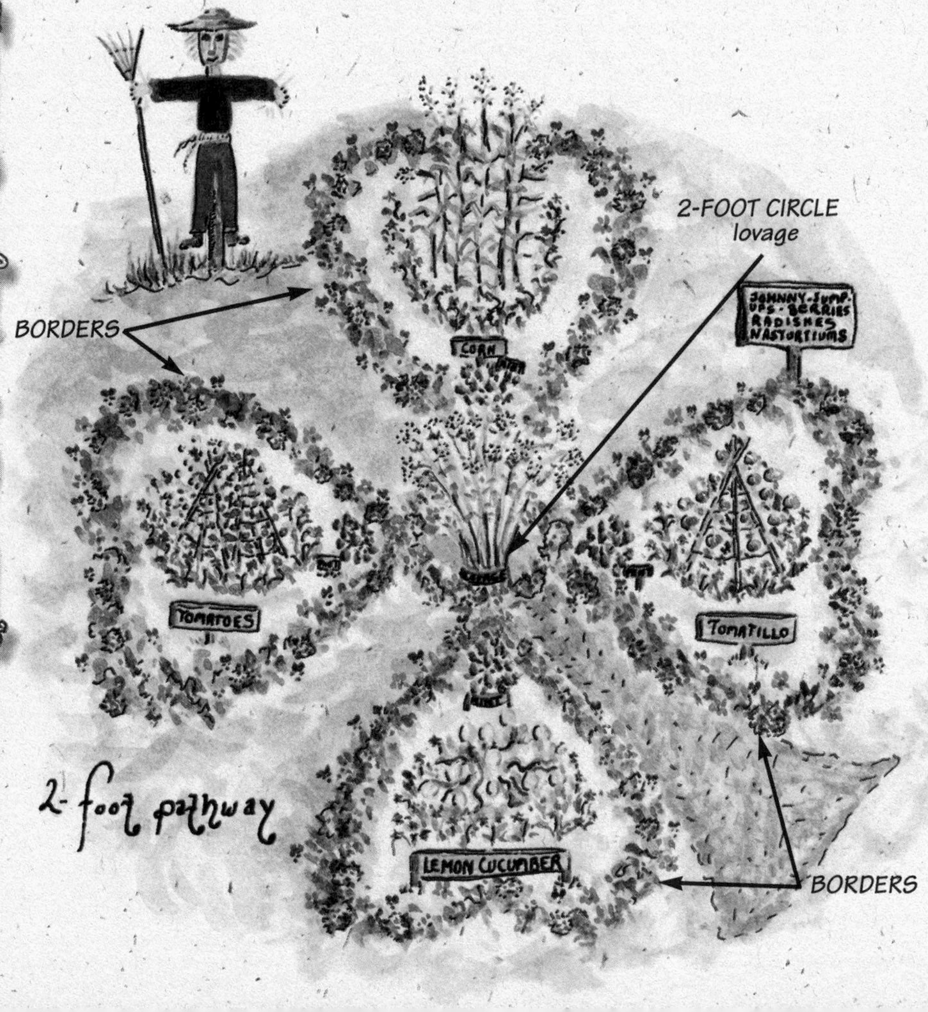

2-FOOT CIRCLE
lovage

JOHNNY-JUMP-
UPS · BERRIES
RADISHES
NASTURTIUMS

BORDERS

CORN

SAGE

TOMATOES

TOMATILLO

2-foot pathway

LEMON CUCUMBER

BORDERS

point and their tips should touch the circle. Leave 2-foot pathways between the shamrock leaves so you'll be able to care for your plants without stepping into the beds. Border the beds with rocks or bricks, and prepare them for planting (see Preparing the Soil, page 140). Work 2 inches of bagged manure into the soil of each section.

Planting & Care

Begin planting when temperatures remain above 65°F. Plant the seedlings in holes twice the width and depth of their root balls. Pretreat the holes with vitamin B_1 (see Planting Seedlings, page 144). Pat soil around the bases of the stems and water gently, directing the spray to the base of the plants rather than the delicate stems and leaves.

Tuck the lovage seedling into the center of the 2-foot circle. Plant the tips of the shamrock leaves with mint seedlings. Members of the mint family are pushy and tend to overrun gardens. To keep

Sunny Days for Growth for Play

10°
55°

Best planting temperature range

Cold Frost, Snow, Wind, Chills, Mint

yours well behaved, slip each seedling into a plastic soil-filled pot with screen-covered drainage holes. Sink the pots into the ground.

Plant the two tomato seedlings 12 inches apart in one shamrock leaf. In a second leaf, use a handful of flour to mark a 2-foot square; sow the corn 6 inches apart in this square, placing each seed in a 4-inch-deep hole. When planted close together in flat ground, instead of a mound, as in the Zuni Waffle Garden (page 121), corn develops tiny, tender ears. Plant the center of the third shamrock leaf with the tomatillo and the fourth with the lemon cucumber.

Scatter the borage seeds around the center plants of each shamrock; press the seeds gently into the soil. Border each bed with a mixed planting of nasturtium, Johnny-jump-up and alpine strawberry seedlings, and radish seeds; alternate them at 6-inch intervals. Press the radish seeds gently into the soil. To ensure a constant supply of tangy radish snacks, sow them every two weeks throughout spring, summer, and fall (except when the temperature goes above 90°F).

SPECIAL CARE

Your newly sown seeds and young plants need a dependable supply of water to get a roothold in the soil. Poke your finger into the soil every day to see if it is dry; water thoroughly but gently if needed. Feed your young plants every two weeks with a half-strength dose of liquid kelp and fish emulsion; after one month, give them a full-strength feeding every four weeks.

Use wooden stakes (at least two per plant) or wire cages to support growing tomatoes, cucumbers, and tomatillos. Pinch off tomato suckers, which are the small stems that grow in the shelter of large ones. These little tykes will take root if you tuck them into soil and keep them moist. Pinch off the tips of fruiting cucumber vines to encourage the growth of fruit rather than leaves and stems.

Fairy Berries

Grown-ups call them Alpine strawberries, but all kids know that these tiny, tart fruits are "fairy berries"—a gift from the wee folk. Look for the first white strawberry flowers; soon they'll develop into ruby red berries freckled with seeds. Eat them quickly— or the birds will.

Sunshine Snack Bar

Go out into your Snacking and Sipping Garden any time you crave a special taste. Eat only the plants, fruits, and flowers suggested here. Don't eat the leaves, stems, or flowers of tomatoes, cucumbers, and tomatillos, which are not good for you.

Strawberry

Rose

Apple

3. All in the Roseacea family.

← Taste me!

The tiny red spots look like the drops of wax once used to seal envelopes — thus the name Cedar Waxwing.

4. Chew on a blue borage flower. Can you identify its taste?

1. Use your fingernail to slit the spur of a nasturtium bloom. Look inside for its hidden cargo of syrup. Sip some. Do you see why hummingbirds love it?

2. Look how corn responds to being crowded!

5. Tomatillos wear stylish paper jackets.

6. For centuries, people used mint as a natural air freshener, strewing it on the floor and walking on it to release its fresh scent. Sniff and taste your mint.

Hoverflies and beneficial wasps sidle in and out of tiny mint and lovage flowers and feed on nectar and pollen. To repay your hospitality, they deposit eggs. These hatch into hungry larvae that devour aphids and other garden pests.

7. Believe it or not, we're all the radish family! Taste us or our flowers.

Cherry

French Breakfast

Black Spanish

Russian

Easter Egg

White Icicle

CHOCOLATE MINT

8. This cucumber got its name from its lemony color and taste.

9. Nibble lovage's leafy tops. They are a great substitute for celery in soups or salads. Snip a tall stem at a node, and look inside. Can you see why these make perfect, edible straws?

Home-Grown Straw

Store-Bought Straw

Slugs are a favorite meal of this young box turtle.

Mother Nature's Tea Party

The pleasure of tending a Snacking and Sipping Garden is that every day is harvest day. Radishes are good-size nibbles just three weeks after planting. Tug them from the ground, rinse them, and eat them on the run.

Summer-Long Harvest

Keep your eye on the corn plants, and start picking when silks peek from the husks. The ears will be just 2 to 3 inches long and

yummy eaten on the spot.

Once you taste cherry tomatoes and crispy lemon cucumbers fresh from the vine, you'll never be able to pass a plant without picking a few. No need to peel the thin, yellow skin from the cucumbers; just eat

them like apples. (One of their nicknames is yellow apple.) Unwrap the little tomatillos from their parchment jackets, and pop the round green fruit into your mouth. Save some for sauces and salsas; they lend a tangy taste.

Sample the flowers of Johnny-jump-ups and borage as well as flowers and the seedpods of nasturtiums while you tend your garden. Add them to salads, sandwiches, cold soups, and dips. Johnny-jump-ups enliven cake toppings and bowls of ice cream. Wrap fairy-size alpine strawberries in the leaves of your chocolate mint for an unbeatable flavor burst.

Radish Sandwiches

Wash and refrigerate radishes for snappy, chilled snacks. For an unusual sandwich idea, use a cookie cutter to make shapes from slices of bread. Butter

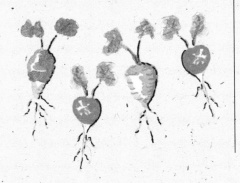

one side of the bread, add sliced radishes, and top with borage flowers. Cover with another slice of bread and serve.

Sun Tea

Harvest a handful of long stems of mint; wash them and place in a two-quart bottle or pitcher. Cover with cold water, and set outdoors in a sunny spot to steep for at least 12 hours. Bring the sun tea indoors, strain, and chill in the refrigerator.

Flower Cubes

Create floating flower jewels for your sun tea. To make clear cubes, boil and cool the water before filling the ice-cube tray. Pick Johnny-jump-ups, borage, mint flowers, and alpine strawberries, and wash them thoroughly. Pour the cooled water into the ice-cube tray, and add a blossom or berry to each cube; put the tray in the freezer.

Just before serving, cut lovage stalks into straw-length sections. Pour the tea over the cubes. Place a straw in each glass and serve with a sprig of mint.

Snack time is any time you're outside in your garden.

their blooms would cure heart problems and sadness. Sprinkle Johnny-jump-up flowers and alpine strawberries on top of scoops of lemon sherbet, and serve.

Heartsease Dessert

Johnny-jump-ups are sometimes called heartsease because people once believed that a tea of

Rainbow Topping

Save all the extra flowers from your borage, nasturtium, Johnny-jump-up, and radish plants. Rinse, then spread them on paper towels to dry. Place them in a pretty bottle to use as a rainbow-colored salad topping.

MOON GARDEN

OUR BEST EVENING HOURS ARE SPENT PLAYING IN THE MOONFLOWER TENT.

FIREFLIES ARE FREQUENT GUESTS; FROGS STOP BY TO EAT AND REST.

STARRY FLOWERS LURE THE MOTHS WHO SIP AND SAVOR SUGAR BROTH.

CATERPILLARS ON A STROLL HIDE FROM TOADS ON FOOT PATROL,

AND UP ABOVE IN BUGGY SKIES, BATS TAKE MOSQUITOES BY SURPRISE.

I f you think that nothing happens in your yard after dark, you're in for a big surprise. Magic happens and miracles unfold when you plant a garden with night-blooming flowers. Under a full moon, your garden looks enchanted, glowing luminously in the night. Critters you never see in daylight stop for snacks; some stay to raise families. And you'll be able to watch it all happening from behind the leafy walls of a vine-covered tent.

Ingredients

INSIDE THE CRESCENT:

2 seedlings, jasmine tobacco

2 seedlings, evening primrose

2 seedlings, four-o'clocks

2 seedlings, evening-scented stock

THE BORDERS:

2 six-packs, white alyssum

2 six-packs, white petunias

2 six-packs, white yarrow

THE TENT:

6 seedlings, moonflowers

rope

5 6-foot bamboo poles or
2-by-2-inch lumber

Fragrance is the color of night. When evening comes in the Moon Garden, pale flowers that look bedraggled and tired during the day lift their heads, open, and release their potent perfumes. Giant, fairylike moths slip from hiding places and follow invisible pathways of fragrance through the moonlight. Bats awaken, stretch their wings, and fly overhead in search of insects. Toads, frogs, glowworms, and fireflies become your guests. Spread out your flowery welcome mat and wait for darkness to fall.

Bat Attitude

Bats have gotten a bad rap for centuries. These gentle bug-eaters aren't after you and won't land in your hair. Instead, they'll rid your yard of hundreds of pesky mosquitoes every night.

Plant moon-
flowers at the
base of each
tent pole.

TENT

Border
plants:
alternate
alyssum,
petunias, and
yarrow

DOORWAY

14

feet

Crescent
interior:
four o'clocks,
jasmine tobacco,
evening primrose,
stock

19

PATHWAY

feet

FURROW

Getting Ready

Select a flat 10-by-10-foot area that gets six hours of sun daily. Outline the area by marking it with a few handfuls of flour along its sides. One of the sides should face directly north. Stand in the center of your plot at noon on a sunny day; the shadow you cast will point north.

MAKING THE CRESCENT

Using the measurements and diagram (opposite page) as a guide, outline a crescent moon shape with flour. Its tips should point north. (The inside arch is 14 feet long; the outside arch is 19 feet.) Follow the outline with a hoe, digging a shallow furrow. Bisect the crescent with a pathway in the middle. Scoop out two more furrows on each side of the pathway.

MAKING THE TENT

To make the tent, you need at least two people. First, lay the five 6-foot poles on the ground. Tie a rope around them about 1 foot from an end. Hold the poles together, tied-end up, and raise them into an upright position in the center of the crescent.

Spread the bottom of the poles apart to make a 4-foot-wide circle. As you do this, the rope at the top tightens and

Snowy Tree Cricket

Mulched floor
4 foot tent
6 feet tall

Mulched pathway

Cricket Thermometers

A snowy tree cricket can help you measure the temperature. Using a wristwatch with a second hand, count the number of times the cricket chirps in 15 seconds and add 40. The total equals the temperature, in degrees Fahrenheit. Compare your cricket calculation to the reading on a real thermometer.

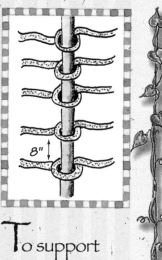

T o support the climbing moonflower vines, wrap rope once around each tent stake, leaving about 8 inches between each row of rope.

stabilizes the tent. Make a doorway on the south side by widening the gap between the two legs facing the path.

To support the moonflower vines as they grow, tie a rope to the bottom of one doorway pole and weave it back and forth around the tent. As you pass each pole, wrap the rope once around it. Spiral from bottom to top, keeping the rows about 8 inches apart. Turn back when you come to the doorway and continue weaving in the opposite direction.

Planting & Care

PLANTING THE MOON

Prepare the beds of the crescent moon for planting (see Preparing the Soil, page 140). Begin planting when temperatures remain above 70°F. Place one seedling of jasmine tobacco, evening primrose, four-o'clocks, and stock in *each half* of the crescent. (Eight plants in all.) The planting holes should be twice the width and depth of the seedlings' root balls. Pretreat the holes with vitamin B$_1$ (see Planting Seedlings, page 144). Slip the seedlings gently into place, then add soil and pat it down.

In the furrows, alternate the border plants—alyssum, petunia, and yarrow—spacing each seedling about 10 inches apart. (Use fourteen border plants for the inside of the crescent arch; eighteen plants for the outside arch.) Plant the remaining four border plants in the furrow along the sides of the path.

Water the plants deeply, directing the spray at the base of the plants, rather than delicate stems and leaves.

PLANTING THE TENT

At the base of each pole, dig a hole twice the width and depth of the moonflowers' root balls. Tuck in the moonflower seedlings, add soil, and water gently.

Little Hands Little Handles

Kids love to help water with child-size watering cans.

Much About Mulch

....

A covering of mulch provides a warm, humid hideout for beneficial insects.

SPECIAL CARE

Mulch the seedlings with a 2-inch-deep layer of straw or shredded bark. For a soft sitting area, spread the mulch on all unplanted ground in the 10-by-10-foot plot.

Each morning, poke your finger through the mulch and into the soil to see if plants need water. Moonflowers are often thirsty, so they usually need water daily. Feed your plants once a week with a half-strength blend of liquid kelp and fish emulsion; after one month, give them a full-strength feeding every four weeks.

As the vines grow, guide them onto the poles and ropes of the tent. Stake the jasmine tobacco, if necessary.

To encourage flowers in the crescent-shaped bed to bloom more, deadhead plants by pinching or snipping the stems at the node just below the worn-out blooms.

Moth Broth

Mash a rotten banana or peach with brown sugar and water to form a thin paste. Pour onto a plate and let ferment in the for two days. Bring the indoors at night. Paint a swath of the broth onto a smooth tree trunk in a dark spot. At night, sneak up and turn on a flashlight.

Evening Stake Out

Snuggle up inside your moonflower tent and wait for the night. Close your eyes, listen to the insects tune up for their evening concert, and inhale the aromas of the opening flowers.

4. Bats harvest their dinners from buggy night skies. They use echo-location as well as their eyes.

Cricket Chorus

This hungry Tomato Hornworm will turn into a beautiful Sphinx Moth

1. At dusk, watch for the evening primroses to open. First there's a shivering movement in the swollen buds, then the pleated yellow petals pop open like satiny umbrellas.

3. Do you hear the hum of sphinx moth wings? If the moths detect a pursuing bat, they dive under leaves for cover.

Jasmine Tobacco

2. Tread lightly on the path, as you look for luminous firefly larvae (glowworms) crawling on the soil.

Caution Glowworm Crossing

5. The giant green luna looks like a fairy who was issued an oversized set of gauze wings. The luna is astonishing and looks astonished, with its two pairs of owl-like wing spots and its long, trailing tail.

6. After sundown the moonflower buds begin to move imperceptibly and the white star-faced flowers open slowly to release a haunting fragrance.

Wingless female firefly

Male firefly

Black & yellow Argiope spider

Magical Moonflower Show Opening Tonight

Four O'Clocks

These old-fashioned flowers open every day about four. Watch for the visits of long-tongued sphinx moths who feed from the trumpet-shaped flowers. If you sit quietly beside the plants, the moths will fly quite near you.

7. Watch male fireflies swoop around flashing brightly. The females stay put and fire an answering flare if they're interested in the male.

8. Use a jar with a screen lid for a firefly lantern. Catch, look, enjoy, then set the fireflies free before the night is over.

Seed-Saving Party

By the end of summer, a tangle of vines covers your tent and bugs and birds have staked out their territories. Stop deadheading flowers to allow the plants to set seed.

Collect the seeds, spread them on a piece of paper, and let dry for a week. Then invite friends over for a seed-saving party. Label and decorate envelopes and write down the planting instructions given here. Pour the seeds into the envelopes and seal. Have friends take home four seed packs to plant their own miniature Moon Garden next spring.

JASMINE TOBACCO:

Cut the oval capsules from the plant, shake out the tiny brown seeds.

ENVELOPE INSTRUCTIONS
After the temperature remains above 65°F, sow the seeds in a sunny spot with rich, freshly raked soil. Dust with more soil. When the plants are 3 inches high, thin to 18 inches apart.

FOUR-O'CLOCKS:

Hold a paper bag underneath the blossoms and shake the plant. Spread the seeds on a piece of paper, and let dry for a week.

ENVELOPE INSTRUCTIONS
After the temperature remains above 70°F, sow the seeds ¼ inch deep in a sunny spot with rich, well-drained soil. When the plants are 3 inches high, thin to 18 inches apart.

EVENING PRIMROSES:

Hold a paper bag under the dried seed heads, and snip the stems so the capsules fall into the bag. Close the bag and shake.

ENVELOPE INSTRUCTIONS
In late spring, sow the seeds in a sunny spot with rich, well-drained, freshly raked soil. Dust with more soil. When the plants are 3 inches high, thin to 18 inches apart.

MOONFLOWERS:

Snip off the round capsule, break it open, and spread the seeds on a piece of paper; let dry for two weeks.

ENVELOPE INSTRUCTIONS
Soak the seeds overnight in warm water before planting. After temperatures remain above 65°F, sow the seeds ¼ inch deep at the base of a trellis. The spot should have plenty of sun and rich, well-drained soil. When the plants are 3 inches high, thin to 18 inches apart.

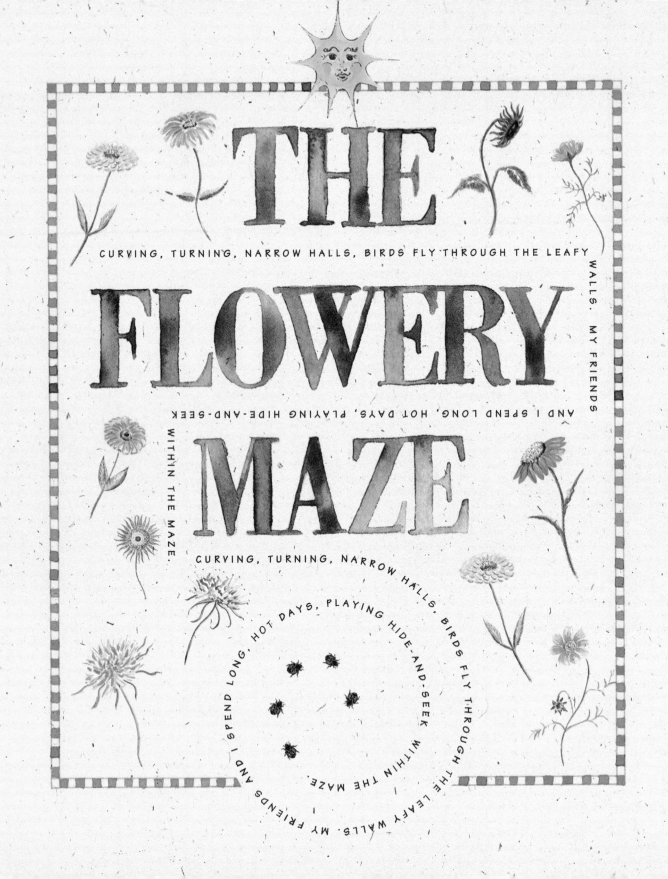

THE FLOWERY MAZE

CURVING, TURNING, NARROW HALLS, BIRDS FLY THROUGH THE LEAFY WALLS. MY FRIENDS AND I SPEND LONG, HOT DAYS, PLAYING HIDE-AND-SEEK WITHIN THE MAZE.

CURVING, TURNING, NARROW HALLS, BIRDS FLY THROUGH THE LEAFY WALLS. MY FRIENDS AND I SPEND LONG, HOT DAYS, PLAYING HIDE-AND-SEEK WITHIN THE MAZE.

Check to make sure that nobody is watching . . . then slip through a small opening in a hedge of flowers and disappear into the secret world of your maze. Crawl through its narrow, curving pathways, trying not to make any false turns, until you reach the inner circle. It's your haven where you can retreat from the rest of the world.

No one can see you, but you can hear everything going on outside your hideaway. Inside, you can be alone with your thoughts, read, write in a journal, or share time with friends.

Towering orange-petaled Tithonia blooms and golden sunflowers, paint-box-colored zinnia, lacy-leaved sweet Annie, and feathery cosmos form the leafy walls of your maze. When the flowers begin blooming, you'll be surprised by the constant comings and goings of wild critters in your maze. Sit quietly, and you may become a part of some real-life garden drama.

Invite family and friends to help you make a stepping-stone art gallery with a collection of flower pictures created right in the ground. Lead guests on

Ingredients

4 seedlings, scabiosa

4 seed packets, 'Autumn Beauty' sunflowers

4 seed packets, Tithonia

2 seed packets, cosmos

2 seed packets, giant zinnias

2 seed packets, sweet Annie

2 40-pound bags aged manure

Friend Not Foe

The flowers of your maze entice an array of beneficial insects into your yard. Friendly wasps cruise flower stalks in search of prey—other insects, not you! Their larvae feast on garden pests, too.

a tour of the creations, which takes them into the heart of the maze.

All summer long and into fall, you'll be able to cut dazzling bouquets from your garden—some to keep and some to share.

Getting Ready

Select a flat 18-by-18-foot area that gets at least six hours of sun daily. To form your maze, you will make three circles, each with a different radius: 3, 6, and 9 feet. Poke a stake into the center of the plot and loosely tie the end of a 9-foot rope to it.

Have your child grab the end of the rope, stretch it to full length, and walk in a circle. You can follow behind with a hoe and use it to outline the circular bed. Repeat this procedure holding the rope at the 6- and then 3-foot points to form two additional circles.

Custom Fit

If your back-yard is too small for the three-ring maze, plant just the two inner rings.

My Mini Maze

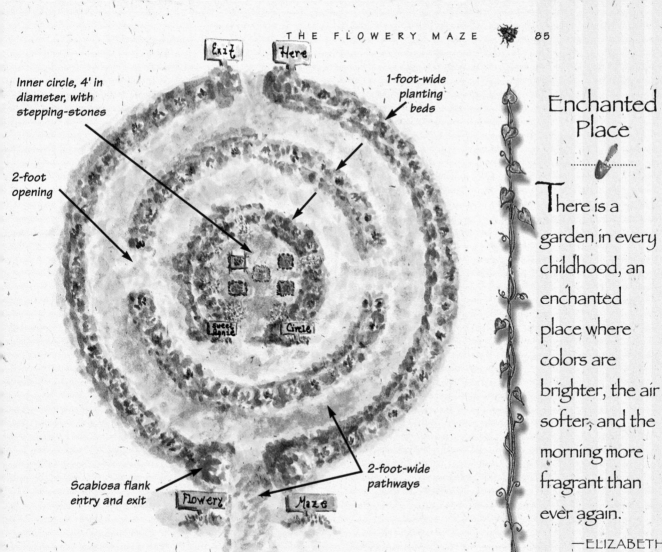

Inner circle, 4' in diameter, with stepping-stones

1-foot-wide planting beds

2-foot opening

Scabiosa flank entry and exit

2-foot-wide pathways

Exit

Here

Sweet Annie

Circle

Flowery

Maze

Each of these rings is the outer edge of a 1-foot-wide planting bed. The remaining areas are pathways. Leave at least one opening in each planting ring so you can move from one section of the maze to another. Prepare the beds for planting (see Preparing the Soil, page 140). Work a 2-inch layer of well-aged manure into each bed.

A little rain and a little sun and a little pearly dew and a pushing up and a reaching out. Then leaves and tendrils all about!

—CHILDREN'S SONG, 1800s

Cosmos & Zinnias

Planting & Care

Begin planting when temperatures remain above 70°F. Flank the two openings of the outer ring with scabiosa seedlings; place them in holes twice the width and depth of the root balls. Pretreat the holes with vitamin B_1 (see Planting Seedlings, page 144.) Then alternate the seeds of sunflowers, zinnias, Tithonias, and cosmos throughout the rest of the rings. When you get to the center ring, add golden-leaved sweet Annie to the lineup. Sweet Annie will infuse your hideaway with a lively herbal fragrance.

Plant seeds 1/4 inch deep every 12 inches, taking care not to plant over the openings in the rings. Pat soil firmly over the seeds, and water thoroughly. (See Planting Seeds, page 141.)

SPECIAL-CARE

Newly sown seeds need to be kept moist to germinate. Each day, poke your finger into the soil in different areas of the maze, and water if it feels dry. Watch for insect or cutworm damage on sunflower seedlings: You may see a few plants that look as if they were chopped off at ground level. Protect them with paper cup collars if necessary (see sidebar, page 21.)

For the first month, feed your young plants every two weeks with a half-strength dose of liquid kelp and fish emulsion; after that, give them a full-strength feeding every four weeks. Always moisten the ground with water before feeding. To prevent mildew, direct streams of liquid at the base of the plants rather than at the delicate leaves and blossoms.

I like to go out on a walk and with each plant and flower talk.

—16TH-CENTURY POEM

Jordan's Garden
Scabiosa
or
Pincushion
flowers

A New Twist

·······❋·······

Our maze is a modern adaptation of a five-thousand-year-old tradition. The first mazes, found in Egypt and on the island of Crete, were probably built of stone. Sixteenth-century Europeans planted low shrubs and herbs in intricate mazelike patterns.

Be sure to keep those greedy weeds from gaining ground. If you pull them out when they're tiny, your beds will stay weed free.

If your tall sunflowers need support, drive a wooden stake at least 12 inches into the soil, and loosely tie the stems to the stake. Use strips of cloth or old stockings as they do not cut into the plants' stems. Scabiosas in bloom sometimes get a bit floppy and need the support of small stakes.

Don't be afraid to cut colorful bouquets from your Flowery Maze. Tithonias, scabiosa, zinnias, and cosmos are exuberant bloomers—the more you cut, the more they will bloom. Just remember to leave enough flowers for the birds and bugs and for your gallery of whimsical, pressed floral stepping-stones.

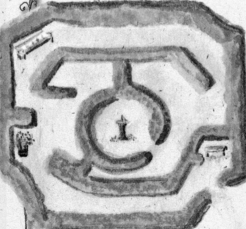

The Little King

Look for grasshoppers near your orange Tithonia flowers. Listen closely for the whirring of wings, the snapping of a jump, or the music the males make when they rub their legs together. Legend tells us that Tithonius, a young king of Troy, slept on bedclothes the color of this flower. The king angered Aurora, the goddess of dawn, who turned poor Tithonius into a grasshopper.

Hide and Peek

Hunker down for a toad's-eye view of your maze. Creep slowly through the winding pathways. Stop, close your eyes, and listen to the rustling of the plants and the conversations of the birds and bees.

2. Find an unopened cosmos and observe it daily. The bud splits open, the petals spread, and the center "disk" flowers open from outside in. Each tiny disk flower then makes a single seed that turns into another flower.

1. Gently run your hands over the scabiosa. Can you see why its common name is pincushion flower?

3. Take time to enjoy the peace and privacy of your maze: no rules, no work, and nobody knows where you are.

4. Rub sweet Annie leaves between your fingers, and sniff their aroma.

5. Zinnias are called "Youth-and-Old-Age" because the flowers last so long. How many different visitors to the zinnias can you record in your journal?

Toe Tasters

You can taste only with your tongue, but a butterfly tastes with all six of its feet and the tip of its proboscis (or tongue).

6. Some people believe that touching and talking to plants makes them grow faster and stronger. Norwegians call this *opelske*, or "loving up." Love up a few plants, and see what happens.

7. Tithonias, zinnias, cosmos, and sunflowers are kissing cousins—all members of one flower family called Compositae.

A FAMILY PORTRAIT

8. With a magnifying glass, search under sunflower leaves for tiny butterfly eggs. Tie a ribbon near the clusters, and visit them every day until the caterpillars hatch.

Stepping-Stone Gallery

Your Flowery Maze will bloom until the first heavy freeze in autumn. After that the maze will look raggletaggle, but resist the temptation to tidy it.

Many helpful garden workers—including beneficial bees and peaceful wasps, as well as the larvae of moths and butterflies—spend the winter in the scraggly stalks and leaves. The garden may not look like much, but it's a cozy home to them!

All through the lazy summer hours, The bees confer amongst the flowers.

compost, and plant another Flowery Maze. You'll likely find that many of last year's flowers have done some of the work for you. They dropped their seeds into the rich earth and will magically reappear in the spring.

Let everything remain until spring. Then uproot the plants or trim them at ground level, add a 2-inch layer of

Flower Gallery

During the late nineteenth century, making exquisitely detailed pictures with pressed flowers was a popular Victorian hobby. Flowers, ferns, and leaves were collected, pressed, and arranged under sheets of glass.

In most cases, these designs were then framed and hung on a parlor wall. Many survive to this day.

Victorian children devised their own version of flower art outdoors. They picked fresh flowers and pressed them right into the soil of their gardens, then carefully covered the blossoms with glass. The ephemeral arrange-

ments became popular and soon appeared in gardens everywhere.

You can create flower pictures in your garden as children did more than one hundred years ago, but for safety reasons, use Plexiglas instead of real glass.

Often, craft stores or framing shops have scraps of Plexiglas that they will give you or sell for a low price. Even tiny pieces make wonderful pictures.

Invite your friends over to create stepping-stone flower pictures leading to the center of your maze, which you can turn into a gallery.

Choose the spots for the pictures. If they are in the shade, they'll last longer. To make a picture, place the Plexiglas on the ground in a pathway, and use a stick to outline the shape. Remove the Plexiglas, and scrape out the outlined area to a depth of 1 inch. Smooth the soil.

Collect a variety of natural materials—mosses, lichens, blossoms, rocks,

pieces of bark, pods, ferns, twigs, and leaves—from your maze and yard. Arrange the objects directly on the soil. If you want to change your design, just lift the pieces and start over.

When your arrangement is complete, set the glass on top of the flowers and brush soil over the edges to seal them. Outline the edge of the picture with small stones, shells, or bark. The picture should last about a week. (Don't worry if the pieces of Plexiglas become scratched from wear.)

Galleries label pieces of art with a title and the name of the artist. You can do this, too. Collect flat rocks or pieces of bark, use acrylic paint to write picture titles for each work, sign your name, and place the labels next to your designs.

I Leave This Notice on My Door
For Each Accustomed Visitor:
'I am Gone Into The Fields To Take What This Sweet Hour Yields'

—PERCY BYSSHE SHELLEY

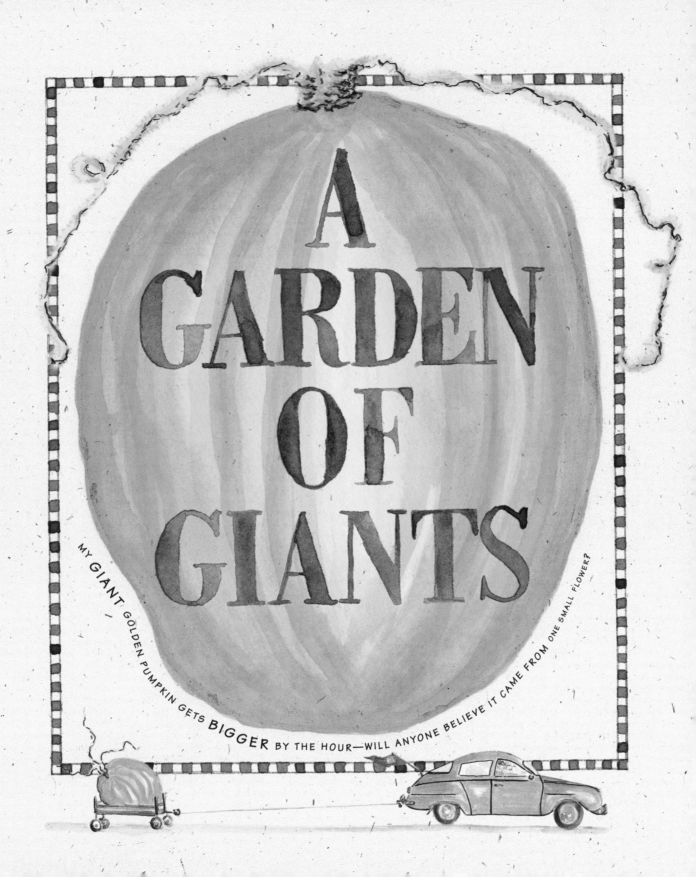

A GARDEN OF GIANTS

MY GIANT, GOLDEN PUMPKIN GETS BIGGER BY THE HOUR—WILL ANYONE BELIEVE IT CAME FROM ONE SMALL FLOWER?

Your friends may think you're telling them a whopper when you describe a pumpkin as big as a bathtub, green beans longer than your arms, and cabbages that turn into walking sticks. Wait until they visit your Garden of Giants and see for themselves. No other garden will ever measure up to this one.

Ingredients

1 seed packet, birdhouse gourds

1 seed packet, yard-long runner beans

1 seed packet, walking-stick cabbage

1 seed packet, 'Dill's Giant' pumpkin

EQUIPMENT:

5 8-foot, 2-by-2-inch poles

50-foot roll of rope

1 5-by-10-foot grid of 10-gauge concrete-reinforcing wire

6 tent stakes

2 40-pound bags aged manure

An arched tunnel, festooned with vines and dangling yard-long runner beans, leads to a tepee hidden under a blanket of leaves. Inside the tent, plump birdhouse gourds hang like pendulums from lacy green walls.

Beside the tunnel and tepee, prickly vines spread a sea of leaves across your yard. Nestled among them are 'Dill's Giant' pumpkins, the king of garden dwellers. Towering walking-stick cabbages stand guard over everything like a troop of slender sentinels.

Throughout the long days of summer, you'll play in a wonderland of colossal vegetables. It may feel like you've escaped to a faraway place inhabited

A Garden Journal

Keep a journal about your garden. It can be a bound blank book or a spiral notebook. Take it into your tepee and record the growth of your giants, draw your favorite plants and insects, or write about the things you discover.

Mini Bottle Greenhouses

Pumpkins and gourds need warm soil to germinate. Make a mini-greenhouse by cutting off the bottom of a large plastic jug. Set it over newly planted seeds. Remove jugs when seedlings appear.

by giants. By autumn, you'll have a bountiful harvest to share with your neighbors. You'll harvest pumpkins big enough to ride in, fashion gourds into birdhouses and bird feeders, and turn cabbages into walking sticks.

Getting Ready

Select a flat 15-by-15-foot area that gets six to eight hours of sun daily. Poke a stake into the center of the plot and loosely tie a 2½-foot string to it. Have your child grab the end of the string, stretch it to full length, and walk in a circle. You or another child can follow behind, outlining the circle with a few handfuls of flour as you go. Stand in the center of your plot at noon on a sunny day; the shadow you cast will point north. Place your tepee here.

To make a tepee, you need at least two people. First, lay the 8-foot poles on the ground. Tie a rope around them about 1 foot from the ends. Hold the poles together, tied-end up, and raise them into an upright

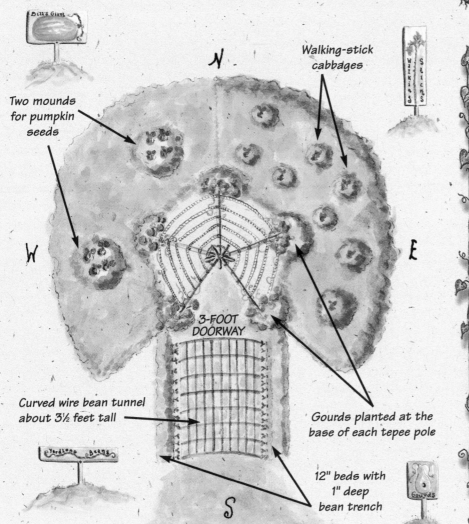

Two mounds
for pumpkin
seeds

Walking-stick
cabbages

Bill's Giant

Walking Sticks

N

W

E

S

3-FOOT
DOORWAY

Curved wire bean tunnel
about 3½ feet tall

Gourds planted at the
base of each tepee pole

12" beds with
1" deep
bean trench

Cardinal Beans

Gourds

Nature's Carpet

To make a soft, dry play area, spread a 3-inch layer of shredded bark or hay on the floor of the tunnel and tepee.

position. Spread the poles apart at the bottom so that they touch the edge of the circle. The two legs that face south are the doorway.

To support the climbing gourd vines, tie the rope to the bottom of one doorway pole and weave it back and forth around the tepee.

Garden Doctor

To prevent the spread of disease, avoid picking beans when the vines are wet. If your pumpkin vines are well-watered and still wilt, look nearby for the entry hole of a borer. Dig it out with a small knife, and wrap the base of the vine with a nylon stocking.

As you pass each pole, wrap the rope once around it. Spiral from bottom to top, keeping the rows about 8 inches apart. (See the illustration on page 74.) Turn back and continue wrapping in the opposite direction when you come to the doorway.

Use the 5-by-10-foot grid of concrete-reinforcing wire to construct a bean tunnel leading to the tepee. Bend the wire along its 10-foot length to form a 3-foot-wide arch. Attach the bottom edges of the tunnel to the ground by hammering the tent stakes over the bottom edge of the wire.

Dig a 12-inch-wide bed along each side of the tunnel. Prepare the bed for planting (see Preparing the Soil, page 140). Make a 4-foot-wide bed around the tepee; top with 2 inches of aged manure and work it into the soil.

Pick Beans on Dry Days

Planting & Care

Begin planting when temperatures remain above 70°F. Soak the gourd seeds for 24 hours (but no longer, or they'll rot) before sowing them. Work your way around the outside of the tepee, making a 6-inch high, 12-inch-wide mound at the base of each pole. Into each mound, poke two 1-inch holes about 6 inches apart. Drop a gourd seed into each hole, cover with soil, and water thoroughly.

Make a 1-inch-deep trench along the base of the bean tunnel. Drop a bean seed every 4 inches, cover with soil, and water the ground thoroughly.

Divide the bed around the tepee into two plots. In the bed facing east, plant walking-stick cabbage seeds about 1 inch deep and 1 foot apart. In the other bed, make two mounds that are about 6 inches high and a foot wide. Poke four

Raising the Roof

On England's Channel Islands, walking-stick cabbages are used as rafters and roof supports for houses. These tall, skinny giants commonly reach 12 feet, but the record holder grew to 20 feet—as tall as a two-story house.

Cabbage Cottage

1-inch holes into the sides of each mound, and drop a 'Dill's Giant' pumpkin seed into each hole. Cover the seeds with soil, and water thoroughly.

SPECIAL CARE

Your giants are thirsty and hungry guys. They need lots of water to reach their maximum size. Every day, poke your finger into the soil near each plant. If the earth feels dry, water thoroughly. If the leaves look wilted at the end of the day, water deeply at the roots of the plants. (Soaker hoses make this job easy and keep moisture off leaves, which can mildew.) Feed your plants every week with a full-strength blend of liquid kelp and fish emulsion. Remember to moisten the soil with water before you fertilize. When pumpkin vines are about 10 inches long, pull out the smallest ones,

leaving only the largest and healthi-
est looking plants. To produce true
giants, leave the two biggest
fruits on each plant and pick the
others. Remove any new fruits
as they appear.

When the gourd vines
reach the top of the tepee, snip
the growing tip to force
growth into the side branches
that produce the female flowers, which
bear the gourds. Take care when working around the vines since they have
shallow roots. Reduce watering in the
fall to harden off the gourds.

Stake the walking-stick cabbages if
necessary, but allow the odd twists and kinks to
remain—they're the plant's personality. When the
stalks are 2 inches thick, start stripping the lower
leaves (toss them onto your compost heap).

Out-of-Bounds

Your giant vegetables will quickly outgrow their garden beds. Allow them to send their vines galloping across the yard, and they will repay you with the biggest harvest in your neighborhood.

Giants Galore

Sneak up on your giants and listen to their conversations with the earth. Lay the head of your stethoscope against the side of a fat pumpkin or on the stalk of a walking-stick cabbage to hear each plant's distinctive sound.

4. Use a soft-bristled paint-brush to move pollen from the stamens of the gourd's male blossoms onto the stigmas of female blossoms. You'll soon be the parent of a bountiful crop of plump gourds.

Do this early in the evening

female

Male

1. With a tape measure, chart the growth of the walking-stick cabbages. Compare their heights to your own. How many inches did you grow this summer?

Side branches have female flowers

Male >

2. Male gourd blossoms form on the main vine, and grow upright on long stalks. The females, which produce the gourd, appear on the side shoots on short stalks.

3. Stretch out inside your tunnel and nibble some of the crunchy beans. Tie a few of the long beans in knots. What happens as they continue growing?

5. Use a nail or a ballpoint pen tip to scratch your name onto the surface of a small gourd. As it grows, so does your name.

OUGH!

Zachary's Garden

6. Run your fingers over the pumpkin vines. Farmers use them to protect the plots of other vegetables.

7. Pose next to your giants at least once a month and have your photo taken.

My pumpkin is gaining over 20 pounds a day!

8. Pumpkins can gain as many as 25 pounds a day! Use a tape measure to see how much they grow each week and record their growth in your journal.

Pioneers made flutes from pumpkin vines

Native Americans made utensils from pumpkin vines

Gifts from the Garden

By late September, your garden is filled with colossal pumpkins, lanky walking-stick cabbages, and long, skinny beans. Everywhere you look, jumbo vegetables are ready to harvest.

Get family or friends together to help you roll pumpkins onto a tarp. Move them to a place of honor—perhaps a porch or patio. In a dry, protected area, they'll last for months.

Cabbages Made for Walkin'

Pull the cabbage sticks from the ground—roots, stem, head, and all—and hang them in a warm, dark area until they are dry and feel lightweight.

Strip off any remaining leaves, and remove the roots. Poke a hole through the top of the stick, and string it with a leather or rawhide handle. Smooth the stalk with fine steel wool, then apply a light coat of varnish and hang up to dry. Walking-stick cabbages make a perfect gift for a friend or relative who enjoys hiking or walking.

Home for the Birds

When their stalks change from green to yellow or brown, gourds are ready for picking. Use clippers to cut them from the vine, leaving some of the vine attached. Clean them with a damp cloth dipped in a weak solution of detergent and bleach. Spread gourds on screens or newspaper in a dry, well-ventilated area. Turn them every few days to prevent rotting.

It is impossible to predict how long it will take each gourd to dry. Small gourds dry faster than large gourds, and gourds with long necks, or "handles," dry first in those areas.

Look for your green gourds to change to soft, pale ivories, browns, rusts, and beiges, sometimes mottled gray. This is a natural part of the drying process and makes each gourd unique. Check the gourds to make sure that they are still firm to the touch. Discard any that feel soft.

Your gourds are dry when they feel light-

weight (remember how heavy they were when you picked them). Some dried gourds rattle when shaken.

Before making a gourd birdhouse, decide which species of birds you'd like to attract. Consult the Appendix (page 152) for the gourd size and the entry hole dimension for that particular species.

Choose a gourd and cut entrances with a hole saw. Scoop out the insides. Fill with water and a handful of gravel, then shake to loosen any remaining pulp. Discard contents.

Drill two small holes at the top of each gourd. Insert a wire through the holes and twist it into a loop to form a hanger. Then drill four 1/4-inch drainage holes in the bottom.

Finish the exterior with a water sealant. Mount your house in a sheltered area at least 5 feet above the ground.

Gourd Container

Saw off the top third of the gourd and remove the dried pulp and seeds. With a sanding sponge, smooth the exterior; wipe it clean and let dry.

Use acrylic paints to decorate your gourd container, or finish with paste wax or varnish, to create beautiful, natural pieces.

Once there was a bumblebee

Who slept till spring had come.

When winter broke, she then awoke

And her wings began to hum.

—EDITH PATCH, 1926

Bumblebee Abode

Drill two holes in the top of the gourd, and insert a wire hanger. Drill four 1/4-inch drainage holes in the bottom, and a 5/8-inch entry hole at a midway point.

Using a wire, stuff with a handful of nesting materials, such as grass or shredded paper. (Keep contents dry.) Waterproof the exterior of the gourd, then hang in an area that's protected from rain, wind, and direct sunlight.

BUZZ INN

My Treasures

I love you and I am your Valentine

My own Moon & Stars & Nickels

MOTHER NATURE'S MEDICINE CHEST

SEEDS AND LEAVES,
ROOTS AND FLOWERS,
ANCIENT PLANTS
WITH HEALING POWERS.

Step inside the fragrant arch of your horseshoe-shaped herb garden and travel back in time. Long before there were doctors and pharmacies, hospitals and nurses, people turned to plants for their medicinal needs. Many of these green medicines are still used today.

Plant a garden of ancient herbs and learn how early healers used them to cure sicknesses and aid in emergencies. At harvest time, you'll be able to fill your own medicine chest with homegrown remedies.

Slit open an Aloe leaf and squeeze the clear gel on your skin. It feels cool and soothing. Use it whenever you have a minor burn or skin irritation.

Ingredients

1 seedling, Aloe Vera
1 seedling, Calendula
1 seedling, catnip
1 seedling, dill
1 seedling, fennel
1 seedling, lavender
1 seedling, lemon balm
1 seedling, parsley
1 seedling, peppermint
1 seedling, sage
1 seedling, woolly lamb's ears
3 seedlings, cilantro

EQUIPMENT:
1 bag shredded bark
2 40-pound bags aged manure

Stuff a pillow with lavender to ensure sweet, colorful dreams, and make your own bandages with woolly lamb's ear leaves.

You'll be able to concoct a lemon balm wash for cold sores, and a healing throat gargle from sage leaves steeped in vinegar.

The petals of golden Calendula will surprise you with their ability to cleanse wounds and heal chapped skin, and a cup of catnip tea may become your favorite sleepy-time drink.

Herbal Sachets

Whenever you clip the herbs in your garden, be sure to save the trimmings. Bundle them together with string and use them as scented "logs" for your fireplace, or snip them into small pieces, dry, and put in sachet bags.

Getting Ready

Select a flat 8-by-8-foot area that gets at least six hours of sun daily. Stand in the center of your plot at noon; the shadow you cast will point north. Outline a horseshoe shape, 6 feet wide and 8 feet long with planting beds 18 inches wide. Make sure the horseshoe opening faces south.

Prepare the bed for planting (see Preparing the Soil, page 140). Top your bed with a 2-inch layer of aged manure, and work it into the soil. Rake the plot smooth. Spread shredded bark in the horseshoe opening to keep down weeds and provide a dry, soft sitting area.

Plant tall dill and fennel at the north end so they don't shade other plants.

Fennel

Dill

Lavender

Cilantro

Lemon Balm

Parsley

Catnip

Sage

Calendula

Peppermint

Aloe

Woolly Lamb's Ear

6' X 8' HORSESHOE-SHAPED BED

3-FOOT INTERIOR

18-INCH BED

18-INCH BED

Planting & Care

Begin planting when temperatures remain above 55°F and after all danger of frost has passed. Start planting 1 foot from one end of the horseshoe, and work your way around to the other end. The holes should be twice the width and depth of the seedlings' root balls. Pretreat the holes with vitamin B_1 (see Planting Seedlings, page 144).

Plant the seedlings, except cilantro, 18 inches apart. Place cilantro seedlings 6 inches apart. Put the tallest herbs, fennel and dill, on the north side.

SPECIAL CARE

Poke your finger into the soil each day to see if it is moist. If it feels dry, water deeply. Feed your herbs once a month with a full-strength blend of liquid kelp and fish emulsion.

Aloe Relief

To ensure a year-long supply of Aloe to put on burns, remove the plant from the ground before the first frost. Pot it in a container, and bring it indoors to grow on a windowsill through the winter.

Herbal Pathways

Your herbs will awaken all your senses. Touch, taste, smell, look, and listen. Get to know the plants and learn some of their powerful healing secrets.

8. If you like the taste of licorice, you won't be able to pass your fennel without nibbling. Fennel is called the weight-watcher's herb because it satisfies an appetite.

Fennel Candy

Benny Spencer's Dill

9. Rub the fuzzy, gray woolly lamb's ears, and you'll understand how this herb earned its name. Healers used this soft plant as a bandage.

1. For thousands of years people used dill to quiet upset stomachs and heartburn. Taste the foliage, flower buds, and seeds.

2. Search through the blooms of the cilantro plant for the small, round seedpods called coriander. Snack on them for a breath-freshening flavor jolt.

Coriander Seeds

Catnip

3. Watch your cat frolic and roll in the catnip. Pick some leaves and stuff them into an old sock for an indoor toy.

7. Rub pungent peppermint leaves on your skin to discourage bugs, or weave a bug-chaser crown out of its long, supple stems.

Peppermint

6. Pick an Aloe leaf, slit it open with your fingernail, and spread the cool gel onto your skin.

Aloe

5. Sit in the middle of the horseshoe, close your eyes, and tune in to the zipping sounds of hummingbird wings, the buzz of bumblebees, and the musical calls of visiting birds.

4. Crush a lemon balm leaf in your hand, and smell its sharp odor and taste its flavor. Beekeepers surround their hives with this herb because it attracts bees.

bees favorite

Lemon Balm

Sage

Hummers

A hummingbird flew past today,

circled my garden and decided to stay.

Its tiny wings made a funny sound,

like zippers going up and down.

It dipped and dived among the plants,

and snacked on spiders, gnats, and ants.

And all day long, for flying power,

it sipped the nectar tucked in flowers.

Home Remedies

Nothing smells better than harvest day in your herb garden. Whenever you brush against a plant or cut a stem, sweet and spicy fragrances surround you.

Harvest your herbs on a dry day. Tie them in small, hand-size bunches, and hang them in a warm, dark place to dry.

Bottled Bounty

Cut stems of fennel, dill, and cilantro. Separate the plants into bunches, and tie them with string. Stick the bunches into small brown paper bags, seed heads first, and tie the bags closed. Hang in a dark, warm area. When thoroughly dry, shake the seeds from the heads and bottle them. Save some fennel and dill seeds for a dream pillow, page 118.

For an upset stomach, put a few coriander, dill, or fennel seeds in a tea ball and drop into a pot of freshly brewed herb tea. (Remove the tea ball or strain before drinking.)

Tummy Tea

Strip dried peppermint leaves from their stems, pack them into a clean tin, and cover with an airtight lid. Store in a cool, dark cupboard.

Herbalists use the healing, anesthetic menthol of peppermint tea to soothe upset stomachs and indigestion. Scoop 2 to 3 teaspoons per cup into a tea ball, place into a teapot, and add boiling water. Steep for 8 minutes, cool, then sip slowly for gentle relief.

Sage Gargle

Sage leaves are filled with astringent and antiseptic tannins that comfort sore throats. Pack a widemouthed jar with whole dried or fresh sage leaves. Cover the sage leaves completely with apple cider vinegar and cap tightly. Store in a cool, dark place, and shake daily. After two weeks, pour the sage-vinegar mixture through a strainer and rebottle the liquid. Put it in your medicine cabinet and use as a gargle for sore throats.

Cold Sore Remedy

Strip dried lemon balm leaves from their stems, and fill a clean glass or tin container. Cap tightly and store in your medicine chest to make an antiviral wash for cold sores. Put 2 to 4 teaspoons of dried herbs in a container, and add 1 cup of boiling water. Steep for 10 minutes, strain, and let cool. Apply the cooled mixture to cold sores with a sterile cotton ball several times a day.

Peppermint
tea
from my
Garden

Herbal Bath Bags

Bath bags are simple to make and can be washed and reused. With pinking shears, cut a piece of fabric into an 8-inch square. Fill the center of the fabric with a handful of lavender flowers and stems and lemon balm leaves, lift the edges to form a bundle, and tie closed with a piece of ribbon. For a muscle-relaxing soak, drop the herbal bag into a tub of hot water. Climb in, stretch out, and breathe in the heavenly fragrance.

Dream Pillow

Aromatherapists and herbalists recommend the sweet, blended fragrances of herbs and flowers for calming, colorful dreams. Mix together dried lavender flowers, lemon balm leaves, and fennel and dill seeds.

Cut a 6-by-12-inch piece of soft fabric and fold it in half. Squeeze a narrow bead of fabric glue (found in craft and yard-goods stores) along two of the edges and allow the seams to dry. Loosely fill the pillow (it should be flat enough to slip inside a pillowcase) and finish closing the bag with another bead of glue.

Slip the thin, fragrant pillow inside your pillowcase and drift off to sleep on a cloud of herb-scented dreams.

ZUNI WAFFLE GARDEN

O, THE FLUTTERING AND THE PATTERING

OF THE GREEN THINGS GROWING,

HOW THEY TALK EACH TO EACH

WHEN NONE OF US ARE KNOWING.

—DINAH MULOCK CRAIKE

Dig into the ancient traditions of Native American gardeners and harvest some of their best ideas for your own backyard. You'll discover the water-saving wisdom and small-space ease of planting a Zuni-style *latdekwi:we*, or "waffle" garden, named because it looks like the breakfast treat. You can build your waffle block by block; start with the four-square version described in this chapter, or think big and create a giant.

Plant some of your blocks with the "Three Sisters of Life"—corn, beans, and squash—in the Iroquois way, using mounds. This important trio of crops help each other in several ways when interplanted. Corn planted deeply in a mound can withstand high winds, and mixed plantings of crops aren't as likely to be destroyed by pests. Corn, the tallest member of the family, provides a support for her climbing sister, the bean. The bean takes nitrogen from the air and transfers it into the soil, enriching it for her two sisters. Squash spreads her big leaves over the ground, shading out sun-loving weeds and helping to conserve moisture for them all.

Ingredients

- 1 seed packet, Indian corn
- 1 seed packet, scarlet runner beans
- 1 seed packet, pattypan squash
- 1 40-pound bag aged manure

Make It Your Own

Grow flowers instead of vegetables in your Zuni Waffle Garden, filling each square with plants that blossom in a particular color. Your creation will look like a patchwork quilt.

The World's Soil

You may be surprised to discover that your backyard has more than one type of soil. There are hundreds of thousands of varieties in the world—over 70,000 in North America alone. Dig up soil in a few different areas of your garden and see how many types you can uncover.

Corn, beans, and squash

tall plants in northern blocks

N

Pathway

Pathway

6"-high mound

4"-high boundary wall

Pathway

Mulch

Getting Ready

To create a four-block waffle, select a flat 12-by-12-foot area that gets at least six hours of sun daily. Outline a 7-by-7-foot square with a few handfuls of flour. Make sure one side of the square faces north. (Stand in the center of your plot at noon; the shadow you cast will point north.) Use flour to mark two more lines that divide the square into four equal blocks.

Hoe or shovel soil from the interior of each block, mounding it along the edges to form hard-packed, rounded, 4-inch-high boundary walls. Prepare the soil for planting (see Preparing the Soil, page 140). Add a few inches of aged manure to each block and work it into the soil. Mulch around the waffle to deter weed growth and conserve moisture.

Planting & Care

Begin planting this garden in late May. Plant the Three Sisters in the two blocks on the north side. This prevents the tall sister, corn, from casting too much shade on the smaller plants, such as the herbs and flowers you may have chosen for the remaining blocks. In the center of each block that you set aside for the Three Sisters, build up a soil hill that's about 6 inches high and 18 inches across.

Water Wisdom

Each small waffle block is a perfect water-catching basin. Not a drop is wasted; it soaks slowly into the ground and into your plants' roots.

Corn is the first sister to be planted. Soak the kernels overnight to soften them. Use a Native American planting stick to poke 4-inch-deep holes about 4 inches apart in the mound. Drop a corn kernel into each hole, fill with soil, and pat down firmly. Water the ground thoroughly.

When the corn is about 6 inches high, add another 2 inches of soil around the bases of the cornstalks. Water gently.

Native American planting stick

Near the base of each corn stalk, make a 1-inch-deep hole. Drop a runner bean into three of the holes and a squash seed in the fourth. Water again.

SPECIAL CARE

The first month of your Zuni Waffle Garden's life is an important one for the germinating seeds and young plants. Check daily for moisture by poking your finger into the soil of each square. If the soil feels dry, fill the block to the brim with water.

Throughout the growing season, feed your plants every two weeks with a full-strength blend of liquid kelp and fish emulsion. Lend a helping hand to the runner beans by guiding their vines up the cornstalks. If the squash vines are crowding the corn, clip them at a node.

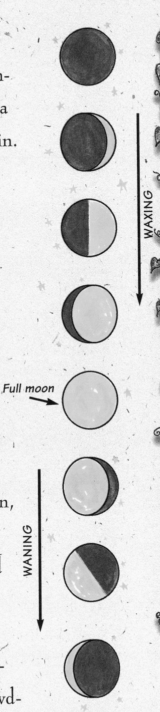

WAXING

Full moon

WANING

Heavenly Help

Some Native Americans plant their aboveground crops, such as corn, on a waxing, or growing, moon. They believe that seeds planted on a waning moon will not grow. They plant underground crops, such as potatoes, on a waning moon.

More Sisters

—

Sunflowers, tepary beans, and pumpkins are another happy trio. Plant the sunflowers as you would corn: one seed in each of four 1-inch-deep holes poked into a mound. When the sunflowers are a foot high, make four more 1-inch holes in the hill. Soak the tepary beans overnight. Place them in three of the holes; place a pumpkin seed in the other. As the pumpkins grow, let them escape the square and roam your yard.

When the corn plants are about a foot high, mound more soil around their stalks to provide support; take care not to bury the young squash or bean plants while doing this.

MUSIC TO THE EARS

Many Native peoples knew the power of "singing the corn into the ground" as they planted. The Papagos walked their fields night after night and serenaded the growing corn, and the Hidatsas sang to their young plants as tenderly as a mother sings to her child. Here's an old Papago song:

THE CORN COMES UP.
IT COMES UP GREEN.
HERE UPON OUR FIELDS
WHITE TASSELS UNFOLD.

BLUE EVENING FALLS.
BLUE EVENING FALLS.
NEARBY IN EVERY DIRECTION
IT SETS THE CORN TASSELS
TREMBLING.

The Birds & the Bees

Take a walk with your "Sisters" and get to know them. Watch how they grow together and help each other through hot, windy days and long, buggy nights.

white Patty-Pan Squash

4 Female blossoms form a fruit after they are visited by pollinating bees

2. Examine the squash vines as they begin to flower. The blossoms with bulb-shaped fruit are the females that turn into squashes.

1. The male corn flowers are shaped like tassels and grow at the top of the plant. The lower-growing female flowers have silks and husks.

← Male flowers

female →

Crows DO eat corn, but they also rid corn of insect pests.

× Toes of the Sky Maiden

4. Gray hairstreak butterflies lay their eggs on corn leaves.

3. The roots of the cornstalk look like toes.

Toes of the Earth Maiden

7. Nibble a few bean blossoms, but leave some to form pods of beans.

Blossoms t; Beins

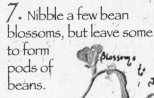

6. Shake your corn until the pollen from the male tassels reaches the female silks. Ears form from the pollinated silks.

raining pollen

Monarchs feist on Sunflower nectar.

Beins turn t; their Sunflower sister fr support.

On the Wing

Spined soldier bugs and minute pirate bugs may lurk around your Three Sisters. Hurrah! These critters and their larvae are great garden helpers; they consume pests that attack and destroy your crops.

5. Here's another "Three Sisters" garden of sunflowers, beans, and pumpkins. Scratch your name into the skin of a young, green pumpkin and watch it grow.

LEA
NORM
MAX
ILYANNA
LILY
ZACHARY

Harvest Celebration

When the corn silks turn brown, the corn is mature. Pick and hang them in a dry area, or spread on newspapers to dry. Harvest the brown pods of the scarlet runner beans and dry them on screens. Gather the squashes, wipe clean, and store in a cool, dry place. They are beautiful displayed in baskets!

Try some of these activities with friends.

Corn Maiden Drawing

Cherokee legends of the origin of corn recount the time when a beautiful lady with silky golden hair, dressed in rustling green robes, came to earth and decided to stay. The maiden's hair is the corn silk; her flowing robes are the leaves; her toes are the prop roots; her arms are the ears of corn waving farewell to her home in the sky. Paint a picture of the Corn Maiden the way you imagine her.

Guessing Game

Break the scarlet runner bean pods apart, take out the beans, and play this Native American guessing game with a few friends. (You can also play it with dried corn kernels or squash seeds.)

Sit in a small circle, and have each player take a stockpile of thirty beans. All players but one close their eyes. That player counts out a few beans from his or her stockpile (no peeking!) and, cupping them in both hands, shakes them close to each player's ear.

Players guess the number and write it on a piece of paper.

Whoever guesses correctly gets the beans plus one bean from each player who guesses

Zuni Scarecrow

The Zuni peopled their cornfields with frightening, human-size figures called the "watchers of the corn sprouts." You can make your own variation of a Zuni scarecrow to watch over the "Sisters."

1. Sink a 2-by-4 pole 18 to 24 inches into the ground.

2. Screw branches into the pole for arms.

3. For the face, fill a cloth bag or pillowcase with straw and tie it closed. Paint a wild face. Glue on corncob rounds for eyes, a stringy mop for hair, red ribbon for a tongue, and cornhusk strips for teeth. Tie the head to the pole.

4. Dress your scarecrow in an old shirt and pants stuffed with straw and tie ends closed. Attach feathers, ribbons, shells—things that will blow wildly in the wind.

incorrectly. If more than one person is right, divide the beans among the winners. If no one guesses correctly, each player forfeits a bean. After everyone has taken a turn, count the beans; the one with the most is the winner.

Indian Corn Jewelry

You and your child can make necklaces or bracelets from jewel-toned Indian corn kernels. Pick hardened seeds out of dried corncobs. Soak the seeds in warm water for at least twelve hours. Use a thick, heavy-duty needle to pierce each softened kernel and string it onto heavy thread or dental floss. Tie a knot to form a circle.

Cornstalk Animals

This craft is for kids aged nine and older, working with an adult.

Cut a dry cornstalk and trim it into pieces, cutting between the knobby nodes to make chunks of various lengths. The length of the piece determines the size of the animal. Use a knife to trim away parts of the stalk, then carve the trimmings into legs, necks, and tails.

These sections must have a sharp point that you can use to insert the piece into the body. Cut a small length of stalk to the size of your animal's head, peel off the outer stalk, and carve the pithy core to shape. Decorate with acrylic paints.

GARDENING
B A S I C S

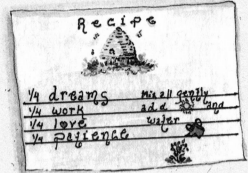

In gardens where grown-ups share adventures and victories with children, there are more things blooming than flowers and trees. Here's what you need to know to make your garden a place where you and the kids grow together.

THE TEN-MINUTE PLAN

Since children can easily feel over- whelmed by long lists of chores or extended work periods, chop gardening time into short blocks.

• Choose a different area each day and work together for ten minutes.

• Celebrate a day of weeding with a ten-minute weeding contest.

• Organize a task force to "uncrowd the plants" with a ten- minute transplanting.

Kids often get so excited about their gardens that they forget about the time, especially if you garden with them. Here are the basic gardening tasks, any of which can be done for ten minutes at a time:

WATERING. I always tell my small helpers that I treat my plants the way I want to be treated. I wouldn't want

to go through a hot summer day without a drink, and plants shouldn't have to suffer through a dry day either. If plants are thirsty, give them a long, deep drink—enough water to soak the ground around them to a depth of at least 3 inches.

Kids love to water. They'll never check to make sure they've satisfied their ten-minute goal with this job. Teach them to do the "poke test" before they water: Push a finger an inch or so into the soil. If it feels dry, water deeply. If it's moist, don't water. When plants sit day after day in soggy ground, their roots may rot. Be sure to direct the stream of liquid at the base of the plants, not the fragile leaves or stems—especially if they are small.

Water early in the morning, so the moisture soaks into the earth instead of evaporating in the hot, midday sun, and don't use any more water than necessary. Collect rain and runoff from the roof of your house in buckets and barrels.

FEEDING. Like people, plants need nutrients to grow. I recommend using organic fertilizers because they break down slowly and provide the plants with a steady supply of nutrients. Examples of organics include compost (see page 145) and aged, bagged manure, which you add when preparing the soil, and liquid kelp and fish emulsion, which you apply during the growing season.

For convenience and health reasons I recommend buying bagged manure for your gardens. This manure goes through a pasteurization process that destroys bacteria and pesky weed seeds.

When fertilizing your plants, always moisten the soil with clear water first. If fertilizer is applied directly onto dry soil, it may burn the plant's roots. Because each garden in this book has its own nutritional requirements, check its chapter for specific feeding instructions.

WEEDS

WEEDING. Stop! Before you pull a weed, examine it and compare it to the plants nearby to make sure it's not one of them. Look at the shape of the leaves, for example, and how they are arranged on the stem.

Pull weeds by hand or use a stirrup hoe, then gather them up and dump them on the compost heap.

DEADHEADING. Children like to deadhead; just saying the word usually elicits a giggle. To help them understand why they're doing this job, explain that plants produce flowers, which bear seeds to ensure future generations. Producing seeds uses energy the

Toolbox

Having a few child-size tools makes it much easier for kids to work alongside you in the garden. Hardware stores and nurseries both carry tools for kids: There are very small-scale sets for preschoolers and slightly larger, heavier ones for school-age children

Tools can be expensive, but good ones are worth their weight in gold. And when cared for properly, they last for years. Here are some basics:

Clippers

Spade

Trowel

Cultivating fork

Lightweight rake for leaves

Shovel

Hoe (an oscillating hoe makes weeding a cinch)

Heavy-duty rake for soil

Watering can

Gathering basket

plant would otherwise spend on blooming. If you clip off a faded flower, you'll stop its seeds from ripening and encourage the plant to send out more blossoms. Give kids a work basket and blunt scissors or clippers, and show them how to cut at a node just below the flower.

At the end of summer, let some flowers go to seed and collect them for next year's garden. Simply hold an envelope under the seed head, clip the flower off its stem and let it fall into the envelope.

MULCHING. Mulch is earth's coverlet, a blanket of organic materials we spread over our gardens to conserve moisture, deter weeds, and prevent erosion. Some common choices are hay, straw, corncobs, wood chips, and aged sawdust.

Spread a 2-to-3-inch layer of

If you can't afford tools, don't worry. For small projects and container gardening, a spoon and fork serve you well. Centuries ago, people tended large fields using only sticks, stones, bones, and shells.

Don't be afraid to break the rules about what to use for garden tools!

mulch around seedlings and on beds. Because these natural materials decompose into the earth, you may have to repeat this process several times during the growing season.

I think of mulching as a ritual of

giving back to the earth some of the nutrients I remove in harvesting. It gives me the same sense of satisfaction I used to feel when I'd tuck my young son into bed under a warm quilted comforter.

CHOOSING A SITE

Most gardens in this book need six to eight hours of sun each day.

Observe your potential garden site in the morning, at noon, and in the afternoon to determine the amount of sunshine it receives.

Try to select a site that is sheltered from harsh winds. Fences, walls, trellises, shrubs, and trees make good windbreaks; however, plant far enough away so that the windbreak does not shade a garden requiring full sunlight.

Stick a shovel in the soil and

Explorer's Kit

Encourage children to discover all of the natural life of the garden—hatching butterflies, nesting birds, pollinating bees, as well as growing plants. An Explorer's Kit should contain:

1. A magnifying glass for viewing the miracles that are often overlooked.

2. A notebook or journal for daily observations, photographs, recording weights and heights of plants, drawings, poems, and descriptions of the garden.

3. A sheet of Plexiglas, on which children can place sow bugs, worms, and insects. They can hold up the sheet to peer at the creatures' undersides.

4. A stethoscope for listening to trees drinking and critters chewing and boring into the bark.

5. A canning jar with a ring lid and piece of nylon screening makes a good observation bottle to catch, watch, and release critters.

6. A measuring tape or **ruler.**

7. A camera for recording momentous occasions in the garden.

8. A flashlight for nighttime exploration.

check for invasions of roots. Plant at least 12 feet away from shrubs and trees as they can be aggressive feeders and will compete for your garden's water and nutrients.

If your site has poor drainage, you may need to add organic materials or consider building raised garden beds.

You've got a good head start if you can find a nice, flat, sunny area already free of weeds and full of loose, organic soil—perhaps a former vegetable garden that you have tended through the years.

Unless you want a secret garden, the plot should be readily accessible—perhaps even visible from the house—so the children will feel close to the daily happenings in their garden.

GET TO KNOW YOUR SOIL

When you and your kids first begin gardening together, you'll have to tackle the challenge of improving your soil and preparing it for future projects. It's the most important step for the success of your garden, so be prepared to dig in. Do you

remember how much fun it used to be to get dirty? Here's your chance to play like a kid again—but this time invite your children along for an underground adventure.

Grab a trowel or shovel, a magnifying glass, a few clear plastic cups, a bucket, and a small hand or two, and head outside to the backyard for a soil expedition. Before you can do anything, you have to get to know the earth in your garden. Tell the kids that even though we walk all over it, take it for granted, and treat it like *dirt,* it is SOIL and our lives depend on it.

Scoop samples of earth from different areas of the garden into the plastic cups. Examine the samples under a magnifying glass, smell them, and feel the textures. Good organic soil that is right for planting looks dark and feels loose and spongy, almost like a great birthday cake. Good earth smells wonderfully toasty and rich. Soils that need improvement feel gritty and sandy, as slick as wet cornstarch, or thick and lumpy like clay. No matter what its condition, your soil can be made better with

Soil is water, air, mineral particles, and organic matter

The Underground Connection

Dig a 10-by-10-inch test hole in your proposed garden site. The sides of the hole offer you a window on the underground world. Crouch down to inspect the layers of earth. The top 6 inches should contain dark organic matter and loads of wriggling critters.

Use your magnifying glass to look for sow bugs, worms, larvae, centipedes, millipedes, and insect eggs in both the hole and the soil you removed. All the organisms you see serve a purpose. Worms and other critters do important jobs, such as consuming pests, tunneling and aerating the soil, and enriching it by redepositing everything they eat in their wanderings.

Unseen by the human eye are billions upon billions of microorganisms—bacteria, fungi, and algae—who do the most important jobs of all. This invisible army of soil workers breaks down the complex molecules of organic matter and turns them into nutrients that plants can absorb. When we feed our soil organic fertilizers and protect it with coverlets of mulch, we send an invitation of welcome to these hungry underground garden helpers.

compost, mulch, and tending. Earth soon responds to care, turning your ground into the fluffy, aromatic material plants need.

SOIL PH. One day at my Heart's Ease Garden, some children were doing a school project—testing the soil to determine its pH. One of the boys asked, "Who cares about pH?" I laughed and told him that I don't and he doesn't, but plants sure do.

I explained that a soil's pH is determined by climate and the types of rocks, minerals, and organic materials the ground contains. pH is a measure of acidity (sourness) or alkalinity (sweetness). It is ranked on a scale of 1 to 14, with 1 being most

acidic, 7 neutral, and 14 very alkaline. (The plants suggested for the gardens in this book thrive in a soil with a neutral pH of 6.2 to 7.)

Soil that is too high in acidity or alkalinity prevents plants from absorbing the nutrients they need for survival. Test your soil with a pH test kit. If the results show that your garden has acidic soil, add bonemeal, wood ash, or lime to bring it back into balance. If the soil is too alkaline, add shredded leaves, bark, aged, bagged manure, and compost.

PREPARING THE SOIL

Outline your proposed site with a long hose or rope. Use a pitchfork or spade to thoroughly loosen the ground inside your garden plot to a depth of at least 10 inches. Then clear the surface of the bed with a heavy-duty rake. Pull out clumps of stubborn grass and weeds, and shake the loose soil back into the bed. Children can't do the heavy labor of clearing the land, but they can help break up clumps of soil and carry weeds and grass to the compost pile. Share the chores and have fun.

Easy Does It

....

Mechanical tilling of the ground damages the soil's structure, exposes micro-organisms to the elements, and awakens a huge crop of sleeping weed seeds. Use hand tools and disturb the soil as little as possible.

Rake the surface smooth, and top with a 3-inch layer of compost and aged, bagged manure—a job kids love! (If you don't have a ready supply of compost and manure, you can purchase these ingredients bagged or in bulk at your local nursery or garden supplier.) Use a pitchfork or a hoe to work the natural fertilizer into the top 6 inches of soil. You can top the exposed ground with a thick, protective layer of mulch composed of leaves and grass clippings.

I tell my young gardeners that soil is a lot like us. Although we can skip a meal once in a while, we won't be healthy if we do it too often. Keep feeding your soil with organic materials as directed in each chapter and you will be repaid with plump, healthy vegetables and brilliant flowers.

PLANTING

Now the exciting moment has arrived: It's time to plant your garden. If you are putting in one of the theme gardens in this book, you can follow the seed-sowing instructions in that chapter.

PLANTING SEEDS

You may decide to design a garden of your own or add your favorite flowers to one of the theme gardens. If so, read the seed packets carefully before planting. Almost all packets have useful information about the correct planting time, how deep to plant seeds, and the number of days until the plant matures and produces its flower, fruit, or vegetable.

If you are planting seeds directly into the ground, make sure the soil is loose and free of big clods, rocks, and twigs. Have your kids stick their fingers at least 6 inches into the soil to feel its consistency. Explain that small roots have to make their way through the soil just as their small fingers do. If the soil is too compacted for fingers, tender young roots will not be able to grow. Break up any remaining clumps of earth and rake the ground.

To sow seeds evenly, pour them into a small grated-cheese container along with a few tablespoons of dry sand. Shake thoroughly to blend the seeds and sand. Scatter a light coating of the mixture across the planting area.

SEED TAPES. If your young gardeners have trouble handling small seeds, use seed tapes, which have seeds attached to their surfaces and are easy for children to manage. You can order seed tapes from catalogs or buy them at nurseries. Kids can also use the strips to form shapes that spell out names or to make pictures on the ground. Sift a fine dusting of soil over the seed tape and sprinkle carefully and thoroughly with a gentle spray of water. The paper will decompose and become part of the earth.

Ancient Seeds

The amazing spark of life cradled inside each sleeping seed can keep glowing for thousands of years. Professor Jane Shen Miller of the University of California, Los Angeles, recently germinated a thirteen-hundred-year-old lotus seed found buried in a dry lake bed in China.

Seed Tapes

Children can make their own seed tapes using the following:

cold water

½ cup of white flour

1 roll of single-ply toilet paper

1 clean plastic syrup container

1 small, clean grated-cheese container

Add cold water to flour and mix until it is the consistency of thin paste. Pour the paste into the plastic syrup container.

Let the kids squeeze the paste along the center of the toilet paper strips. Fill the empty cheese container with the small, hard-to-handle seeds and sprinkle them directly onto the moist paste strips. Lay the strips of toilet paper in your seedbed in desired lengths and designs.

Seeds

Paste

STARTING INDOORS

You can get a jump on spring by starting seeds indoors on sunny windowsills or under a forty-watt incandescent bulb. Spoon bagged sterile potting soil into empty egg cartons or into multi-sectioned flats or peat pots, which you can buy at a garden center. Sow the seeds at the time and depth indicated on the seed packet. Cover with a sprinkling of soil. Water gently so as not to disturb the seeds. Each day, poke your finger carefully into the soil. Water if it feels dry.

Seeds started indoors need to be introduced slowly to the climate outdoors; this process is called hardening off. After the seedlings produce their first adult leaves, which look very different from the initial pairs of baby leaves, stop fertilizing and water as needed. Move the young plants to a shady, sheltered area outside for a few hours a day, and gradually increase the time. Bring them indoors at night.

After about a week, place the plants in a sunny spot outdoors, but continue to bring them inside at night. When temperatures are warm enough (check the seed packets for this information), leave them outside day and night for a week, then transplant them to their new homes in the garden.

PLANTING SEEDLINGS

Water seedlings before you plant them, whether you grew them yourself or purchased them at a nursery. If the seedlings are growing in flats or egg cartons, use a spoon to lift out the soil ball. Don't pull the plant out by the tender stem—it will break. Be sure to dig a hole that's twice the width and depth of the root ball.

Plants need vitamins too! Use vitamin B_1 (available in nurseries and garden centers) whenever you transplant seedlings into your garden. This vitamin stimulates root growth and eases your seedling through the trauma of transplanting. Fill your planting hole with B_1 and water, let drain, then slip in your tender seedling. Add soil, tamp it down, and water again.

If you have used peat pots, moisten the young plants and set both container and plant into a hole that's been pretreated with vitamin B_1. Tamp down the soil and water.

CONTAINER GARDENING

Introduce children to gardening by encouraging them to plant a miniature garden of small, easy-to-care-for container-grown plants. Here are a. few basic tips for successful container gardening.

1. Plants like living in a clean place. Before using a container, scrub it with warm soapy water and rinse it thoroughly. If you don't, your plants may develop diseases.

2. Water and air need to pass through the soil to keep the plants healthy. Check to see whether the containers have drainage holes. If they don't, drill some holes in the bottoms. Cover the openings with nylon-mesh screening (it cuts more easily than wire mesh) so the soil doesn't wash out when you add water. Fill the containers to 1 inch below the rim with bagged sterile

potting soil. You can plant either seeds or seedlings in pots.

3. Treat container-grown plants to doses of organic fertilizer or compost. Water only when the top 2 inches of soil feel dry (check by poking with your finger). Overwatering and poor drainage are as damaging to plants as leaving them hungry and thirsty.

COMPOST: GARDEN HEALTH FOOD

You can "grow your own soil" by starting a compost pile and feeding your garden with the finished product. To learn what compost is, go outside with the kids and scoop up a layer of fallen leaves and soil. Spread these goodies on a newspaper: Smell them, feel them, and take a close look at them. This decaying organic matter is compost—the perfect soil conditioner.

When living matter rots and returns to the earth, it improves the structure of the soil, balances the pH, and keeps both plants and underground garden helpers supplied with food.

Humus is the rich, black end product of composting—the stuff at the bottom of your heap. Because it is so valuable to soil and plants, it is called the "Earth Nurse." Humus, which does its work inside the soil itself, and mulch, which protects the soil from above, are a wonderful rotten twosome that work together to improve your garden.

A HEALTHY HEAP

When you compost, you are giving Mother Nature a helping hand by speeding up the natural process of decomposition that usually takes a full year to accomplish. If everyone composted, our soil would be healthier, and our landfills wouldn't be overflowing.

In the world of compost, bigger is better. If you have a mass of decomposing matter that's at least 3 feet high, wide, and deep, the pile heats up, stays hot, and rots faster. All kinds of vegetable matter—fruit and vegetable peels, grass, leaves, and twigs—belong in a compost heap. Yours will grow quickly with material you once threw out with the trash.

If you're starting a heap

from scratch, add the ingredients in 3-to-4-inch-thick layers. At the bottom, place dry stalks or twigs to provide drainage and allow air to circulate. Alternate fine-textured materials, such as vegetable peelings, flower clippings, and grass, with coarse-textured items, such as leaves, cornstalks, and twigs.

Supercharge your heap—which is like a giant health-food sandwich—with organic fertilizers, such as manure, rock phosphate, or bonemeal.

The bacteria and fungi in a compost pile need water and air to do their job. To make sure they have the right amount of moisture, stick your hand into the pile and squeeze. If the compost feels like a moist sponge, it is perfect. If the compost is dry, use a hose or watering can to wet the pile. If the heap begins to smell rotten, add air by turning chunks of compost with a pitchfork.

The compost is "done" when it is a fluffy, black material. Spread it on your garden, and make your plants happy.

COMPOST SANDWICH

BUILDING A COMPOST BIN. A wire enclosure is one of the most common types of compost bin and it's very easy to make. Purchase a roll of 3-foot-wide garden fencing with 2-by-4-inch holes. Use wire cutters to cut a 10-foot length from the roll to make a bin 3 feet in diameter. Form the bin by fastening the ends of the fencing together with short pieces of wire.

You can easily moisten and aerate the contents of such an enclosure. To remove the compost, simply lift up the wire. It's easy to keep 3 or 4 bins going at the same time. The contents of a bin quickly turn into compost. Once the first bin is full, move on to the next.

BINS TO BUY. Many nurseries and garden catalogs offer polyethylene units with snap-on lids; these bins create finished compost in just weeks. Some have special channels to maintain moisture and add air, while others are drums that need periodic rotation to mix the contents. Check Resources, page 153, for suppliers.

WORM MAGIC

One day, I dropped by a friend's house to admire his gardens. When I asked him the secret of his success, he took my hand, led me to a large concrete box, and lifted the lid. Inside was a wriggling mass of shiny red earthworms. "Now you know my secret," he said. "And I am going to fill a bucket with worms for your garden."

Since that day, my best garden helpers have been the huge family of worms that grew from my friend's gift. They live in a special bin my husband and I built for them. My human family is treated to regular worm updates, and they sometimes call me "mother of millions."

Earthworms are the magicians of the underground. While they quest for food, they slip accordion-like through the soil, eating debris and pooping it out as a rich natural fertilizer called castings. As they slither through the soil, they leave behind nutritious, nitrogen-rich slime and create a vast underground network of tunnels, which aerate the soil and allow plant roots to breathe and grow.

Dirt About Worms

....

- One pound of worms eats ½ pound of kitchen scraps each day.

- A worm can move a rock that's 60 times its own body weight. (That's like you lifting a truck.)

- There are more than 2,400 species of earthworms; they range in length from ⅕ inch to 22 feet (South Africa's Microhaetus rappi).

- Worms breathe through their skin.

- A worm can live for 12 years.

- Worms are hermaphroditic, which means each one has both male and female reproductive organs; however, it takes two worms to reproduce.

- Worms produce as many as 1,500 offspring a year.

- The body of a worm is made of 100–200 ringed segments; undulating muscles move it through the soil.

- According to some German scientists, earthworms actually sing in a definite and changing rhythm.

All you have to do is provide your worms with a few basic necessities: a secure home, food (your garbage is their gourmet feast), and moisture.

BUILDING A WORM BOX

Situate your worm box in a shady area against a fence or beside a sheltering wall. Use exterior-grade plywood to build a bottomless box at least 4 feet square and 1 foot high. Cut a piece of plywood for a lid. Separate your box into two sections with a solid center divider.

Layer the bottom with a few inches of moist soil and some kitchen scraps. Gently add your worms to their new home and cover them with a topping of clippings or soil.

Make a habit of

topping the worms with soil, clippings, or wet newspaper whenever you feed them. Sprinkle with water and close the lid.

Fill one side of the box before moving to the other. Dig into the full section to check your worms' progress. If most of the food is unidentifiable and resembles loose, dark soil, the worms are working their wizardry. Use a trowel or shovel and fill a bucket with the worms' offerings and spread it around your plants.

You can buy earthworms by the pound (1,000 per pound) at nurseries or bait shops, or through mail-order catalogs (see Resources, page 156).

Appendix

THE PIZZA PATCH CHAPTER

Pat Reppert's Wonderful Pizza Sauce

(Makes 1 quart of sauce)

2½ pounds Roma tomatoes (about 12 to 15 small)

4 tablespoons olive oil

2 onions, peeled and sliced

3 cloves garlic, peeled and cut into slivers

1 zucchini (do not peel)

2 bell peppers, cored, seeded, and diced

1 teaspoon salt

½ teaspoon black pepper

1 tablespoon sugar

3 tablespoons fresh basil leaves, chopped

1 tablespoon fresh oregano leaves, chopped

2 1-inch sprigs fresh rosemary, chopped

1. Cut tomatoes into quarters. Have your child squeeze the tomatoes into a 3-quart saucepan. Combine tomatoes, juice, and seeds in the same pan. Cover and cook over medium-low heat for 10 minutes, stirring frequently to prevent sticking.

2. When tomatoes become soft, use a large spoon to separate and crush them. Cook, uncovered, over low heat for 15 minutes, stirring frequently.

3. Pour the cooked tomatoes into a food mill to remove seeds and skins or pulse gently in a food processor. Set tomatoes aside.

4. Heat oil in a 3-quart saucepan over medium heat. Add onions and cook, stirring frequently until softened and golden-colored. Make a well in the center of the onions and add the garlic. Cook 1 to 2 minutes, stirring to avoid burning.

5. Add the zucchini, bell peppers, salt, pepper, and sugar. Cook, covered, over low heat for 5 minutes, stirring frequently. Then add the milled tomatoes and continue cooking, uncovered, for 30 minutes, stirring frequently to prevent burning.

6. Add the basil, oregano, and rosemary and cook 10 minutes more, until sauce thickens. Let the sauce cool, then add salt to taste. Refrigerate for 24 hours before using. The sauce will develop deeper flavor and thicken a bit more.

NOTE: Cooking times vary according to juice content in tomatoes.

New Basics Pizza Dough

Makes four 6-inch pizzas*

1 cup warm water (105° to 115°F)
1 package active dry yeast
2½ to 3 cups unbleached
 all-purpose flour
2 tablespoons olive oil
½ teaspoon salt

1. Combine water, yeast, and 1½ cups of flour in a large bowl. Mix well. Gradually add oil, salt, and remaining flour. With your hands or a wooden spoon, combine ingredients until dough holds its shape.

2. Place dough on a lightly floured surface and knead until it is smooth and elastic, 5 minutes. If dough becomes sticky, sprinkle a bit more flour over it.

3. Transfer dough to a lightly oiled 2-quart bowl. Cover bowl with plastic wrap, and let dough rise until it has doubled in size, about 1 hour.

4. Place covered bowl in the refrigerator overnight.

5. An hour before the kids arrive, remove dough from the refrigerator and preheat the oven to 500°F. Punch a hole in center of the slightly risen dough. Let rise for another hour. On a lightly floured surface, divide into 4 pieces and roll them into balls. It's ready for the kids to shape, decorate, and bake (see page 26).

*For a larger crowd, make two batches.

A GARDEN OF GIANTS CHAPTER

GOURD BIRDHOUSES

BIRD	Gourd (width)	Hole Size	Entry Hole Height	Special Instructions
BLUEBIRD	5"	1 3/8"	8"	Mount at edge of clearing
CHICKADEE OR WREN	4"	1 1/8"	7"	Layer floor with wood shavings
NUTHATCH	4"	1 3/8"	7"	Layer floor with wood shavings
TITMOUSE	4"	1 1/4"	7"	Layer floor with wood shavings
TREE SWALLOW	5"	1 1/2"	5"	Mount at edge of clearing

Resources

Seed Companies, Nurseries & Catalogs

Applesource
1716 Apples Road
Chapin, IL 62628
(800) 588-3854 Orders
(217) 245-7589 Customer
  service
(217) 245-7844 Fax
www.applesource.com
vorbeck@csj.net

Burpee Gardens
300 Park Avenue
Warminster, PA 18991-0001
(800) 888-1447 Orders
(800) 487-5530 Fax
www.burpee.com
burpees@surfnetwork.net

Cook's Garden
P.O. Box 5010
Hodges, SC 29653-5010
(800) 457-9703 Orders and
  customer service
(800) 457-9705 Fax
www.cooksgarden.com
snoflake@sover.net

Daffodil Mart
30 Irene Street
Torrington, CT 06790
(800) ALL-BULB
  (255-2852) Orders
(800) 420-2852 Fax

Dutch Gardens
P.O. Box 200
Adelphia, NJ 07710-0200
(800) 818-3861 Orders
(800) 775-2852 Customer
  service
(732) 780-7720 Fax
www.dutchgardens.nl
cs@dutchgardens.nl

Edible Landscaping
P.O. Box 77
Afton, VA 22920-0077
(800) 524-4156 Orders
(804) 361-9134 Customer
  service
(804) 361-1916 Fax
www.eat-it.com
el@cstone.net

Ferry-Morse Seeds
P.O. Box 488
Fulton, KY 42041-0488
(800) 283-3400 Orders
(800) 283-6400 Customer
  service
(800) 283-2700 Fax
www.gardennet.com/
ferrymorse
catalog@ferrymorse.com

Forestfarm
990 Tetherow Road
Williams, OR 97544-9599
(541) 846-6963
www.forestfarm.com
forestfarm@aonepro.net

Gardens Alive!
5100 Schenley Place
Lawrenceburg, IN 47025
(812) 537-8650 Orders
(812) 537-8651 Customer
  service
(812) 537-5108 Fax
76375.2160@compuserve.com

Goodwin Creek Gardens
P.O. Box 83
Williams, OR 97544
(800) 846-7359 Orders
(541) 846-7357 Customer
  service and fax

Gourmet Gardener
8650 College Boulevard
Overland Park, KS 66210-1806
(913) 345-0490 Orders
(913) 451-2443 Fax
www.gourmetgardener.com
information@gourmetgar-
dener.com

Gurney's Seed & Nursery Co.
110 Capital Street
Yankton, SD 57079
(605) 665-1930 Orders
(605) 665-1671 Customer
  service
(605) 665-9718 Fax
www.gurneys.com
info@gurneys.com

Heirloom Old Garden Roses
24062 Riverside Drive N.E.

St. Paul, OR 97137
(503) 538-1576 Orders
(503) 538-5902 Fax
Catalog $5

Henry Field's Seed &
Nursery Co.
415 North Burnett
Shenandoah, IA 51602-0001
(605) 665-9391 Orders
(605) 665-4491 Customer
    service
(605) 665-2601 Fax
www.henryfields.com
info@henryfields.com

High Country Gardens
2902 Rufina Street
Santa Fe, NM 87505-2929
(800) 925-9387 Orders
(505) 925-9387 Customer
    service
(800) 925-0095 or
(505) 438-9552 Fax
www.highcountrygardens.com
plants@highcountrygardens.com
Perennial plants

Irish Eyes with a Hint of Garlic
P.O. Box 307
Ellensburg, WA 98926
(509) 925-6025 Orders and
    customer service
(509) 925-9238 Fax
www.irish-eyes.com
    potatoes@irish-eyes.com
    Handles inquiries by
    mail only

Johnny's Selected Seeds
1 Foss Hill Road
RR1 Box 2580
Albion, ME 04910-9731
(207) 437-4395 Orders
(207) 437-9294 Customer
    service
(800) 437-4290 or
(207) 437-2165 Fax
www.johnnyseeds.com
commercial@johnnyseeds.com

K. Van Bourgondien & Sons
P.O. Box 1000
Babylon, NY 11702-9004
(800) 552-9996 Orders
(800) 552-9916 Customer
    service
(516) 669-1228 Fax
www.dutchbulbs.com
blooms@dutchbulbs.com

Kids in Bloom
P.O. Box 344
Zionsville, IN 46077
(317) 636-3977 Orders
(317) 916-9033 Fax
Chemical-free seeds grown by
kids. Profits benefit children.
Seed Guardian Project for
educators and parents

Liberty Seed Company
P.O. Box 806
461 Robinson Drive S.E.
New Philadelphia, OH
44663-0806
(800) 541-6022 Orders
(330) 364-1611 Customer
    service
(330) 364-6415 Fax
www.libertyseed.com
info@libertyseed.com

Lilypons Water Gardens
6800 Lilypons Road
Buckeystown, MD 21717-
    0010
(800) 365-5459 Orders and
    customer service
(800) 879-5459 Fax
www.lilypons.com
info@lilypons.com

Logee's Greenhouses
141 North Street
Danielson, CT 06239
(860) 774-8038 Orders
(888) 774-9932 Fax
http://logees.com/www/
logee-info@logees.com

McClure & Zimmerman
P.O. Box 368
108 West Winnebago
Friesland, WI 53935-0368
(800) 883-6998 Orders
(800) 692-5864 Fax
www.mzbulb.com

Milaeger's Garden
4838 Douglas Avenue
Racine, WI 53402-2498
(800) 669-9956 Orders and
    customer service
(414) 639-1855 Fax
www.milaegersgardens.com
Mail-order via Internet
only—no catalog

Mountain Valley Growers
38325 Pepperweed Road
Squaw Valley, CA 93675
(209) 338-2775 Orders
(209) 338-0075 Fax
www.mountainvalleygrowers.com
mvg@spiralcomm.net
Plants only

Native Seeds/SEARCH
526 N. 4th Avenue
Tucson, AZ 85705
(520) 622-5561 Orders and
    customer service
(520) 622-5591 Fax
http://desert.net/seeds/home.htm
jhosofaz@aol.com

Natural Gardening Company
217 San Anselmo Avenue
San Anselmo, CA 94960
(707) 766-9303 Orders and
    customer service
(707) 766-9747 Fax
(415) 456-5060 Store
www.naturalgardening.com
info@naturalgardening.com

Nichols Garden Nursery
1190 N. Pacific Highway N.E.
Albany, OR 97321-4580
(541) 928-9280 Orders and
    customer service
(800) 231-5306 or
(541) 967-8406 Fax
www.gardennursery.com
info@gardennursery.com

Nor'East Miniature Roses, Inc.
P.O. Box 307
Rowley, MA 01969-0607
(800) 426-6485 Orders
(978) 948-7964 Customer
    service
(978) 948-5487 Fax
www.noreast-miniroses.com
nemr@shore.net

Old House Gardens
536 West Third Street
Ann Arbor, MI 48103-4957
(734) 995-1486 Orders
(734) 995-1687 Fax

www.oldhousegardens.com
OHGBulbs@aol.com
Heirloom bulbs from 1200s
    to 1940s

One Green World
28696 South Cramer Road
Molalla, OR 97038-8576
(503) 651-3005 Orders
(800) 418-9983 Fax
www.onegreenworld.com
ogw@teleport.com

Park's Countryside Gardens
1 Parkton Avenue
Greenwood, SC 29647-
    0001
(800) 845-3369 Orders
(864) 223-8555 Customer
    service
(800) 275-9941 Fax
www.parkseed.com
orders@parkseed.com

Peaceful Valley Farm Supply
P.O. Box 2209
Grass Valley, CA 95945
(530) 272-4769 Orders
(530) 272-4794 Fax
www.groworganic.com
catalog@groworganic.com
Everything organic, bene-
    ficial insects

Pinetree Garden Seeds
P.O. Box 300
New Gloucester, ME 04260
(207) 926-3400 Orders
(888) 52-SEEDS Fax
www.superseeds.com
superseeds@worldnet.att.net

Redwood City Seed Co.
P.O. Box 361

Redwood City, CA 94064
(650) 325-7333 Orders
(650) 325-4056 Fax
www.ecoseeds.com

Richters Herbs
357 Highway 47
Goodwood, Ontario, Canada
    LOC1A0
(905) 640-6677 Orders
(905) 640-6641 Fax
www.richters.com
orderdesk@richters.com

Seed Savers Exchange
3076 North Winn Road
Decorah, IA 52101
(319) 382-5990 Orders

Seeds Blum
HC 33 Idaho City Stage
Boise, ID 83706-9725
(800) 528-3658 Orders
(800) 742-1423 Customer
    service
(208) 338-5658 Fax
www.seedsblum.com
103774.167@compuserve.com

Seeds of Change
P.O. Box 15700
Santa Fe, NM 87506-5700
(888) 762-7333 Orders
(888) 329-4762 Fax
www.st4.yahoo.com/seeds
    ofchange
gardener@seedsofchange.com
Certified organic

Select Seeds
180 Stickney Road
Union, CT 06076-4617
(860) 684-9310 Orders
(800) 653-3304 Fax

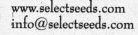

www.selectseeds.com
info@selectseeds.com

Shepherd's Garden Seeds
30 Irene Street
Torrington, CT 06790-6658
(860) 482-3638 Orders
(860) 482-0532 Fax
www.shepherdseeds.com

Sonoma Antique Apple Nursery
4395 Westside Road
Healdsburg, CA 95448
(707) 433-6420 Orders
(707) 433-6479 Fax
www.applenursery.com
tuyt20b@prodigy.com

Southern Exposure Seed
Exchange
P.O. Box 170
Earlysville, VA 22936
(804) 973-4703 Orders
(804) 973-8717 Fax
www.southernexposure.com
Catalog $2

Stokes Seeds, Inc.
P.O. Box 548
Buffalo, NY 14240-0548
(800) 396-9238 Orders
(888) 834-3334 Fax
www.stokeseeds.com
stokes@stokeseeds.com

Territorial Seed Company
P.O. Box 157
Cottage Grove, OR 97424-
    0061
(541) 942-9547 Orders and
    customer service
(888) 657-3131 Fax
www.territorial-seed.com
tertrl@srv1.vsite.com

Thompson & Morgan
P.O. Box 1308
Jackson, NJ 08527-0308
(800) 274-7333 Orders and
    customer service
(888) 466-4769 Fax
www.thompson-morgan.com

Tomato Growers Supply
Company
P.O. Box 2237
Fort Myers, FL 33902
(941) 768-1119 Orders and
    customer service
(941) 768-3476 Fax

Wayside Gardens
1 Garden Lane
Hodges, SC 29695-0001
(800) 845-1124 Orders
(800) 457-9712 Fax
www.waysidegardens.com
gardener@waysidegardens.com

William Tricker, Inc.
7125 Tanglewood Drive
Independence, OH 44131
(800) 524-3492 Orders
(216) 524-3491 Customer
    service
(216) 524-6688 Fax
www.tricker.com
Water gardens

Wood Prairie Farm Maine
Potato Catalog
49 Kinney Road
Bridgewater, ME 04735
(800) 829-9765 Orders
(207) 429-9765 Customer
    service
(800) 300-6494 Fax
www.woodprairie.com

info@woodprairie.com
Certified organic

Worm Resources

Cape Cod Worm Farm
30 Center Avenue
Buzzard's Bay, MA 02532
(508) 759-5664 Customer
    service and fax
http://members.aol.com/cape-
worms/private/wormhome.htm
capeworms@aol.com

Flowerfield Enterprises
10332 Shaver Road
Kalamazoo, MI 49024-6744
(616) 327-0108
(616) 327-7009 Fax
http://www.wormwoman.com
nancy@wormwoman.com
Flowerfield offers worms,
books, and a fabulous recy-
cled plastic bin for worm
composting.

Worm Digest
P.O. Box 544
Eugene, OR 97440-0544
(541) 485-0456 Customer
    service and Fax
http://www.wormdigest.org
mail@wormdigest.org
Worm Digest is a project of
Edible City Resource Center,
a 501(c)3 nonprofit organi-
zation. Supplies, books, and
a quarterly newsletter $12/yr.

Organizations & Suppliers

American Community
Gardening Association
100 North 20th Street
5th Floor
Philadelphia, PA 19103-1495
(215) 988-8785
(215) 988-8810
http://communitygarden.org
smccabe@pennhort.org

American Horticultural Society
7931 East Boulevard Drive
Alexandria, VA 22308-1300
(800) 777-7931
www.ahs.org

Arizona Biological Control,
Inc. (Arbico, Inc.)
P.O. Box 4247
Tucson, AZ 85738-1247
(800) 767-2847
(520) 825-9785 Customer
   service
(520) 825-2038 Fax
www.arbico.com
arbico@aol.com
Insectary

Bat Conservation International
P.O. Box 162603
Austin, TX 78716-2603
(800) 538-BATS (2287)
(512) 327-9721 Customer
   service
(512) 327-9724 Fax
www.batcon.org
batinfo@batcon.org

Butterfly Gardeners' Quarterly
P.O. Box 30931
Seattle, WA 98103

No calls, please
www.butterflygardens.com
skippers@scn.org
Butterfly newsletter $10/yr.

Gardener's Supply Company
128 Intervale Road
Burlington, VT 05401-2850
(800) 863-1700
(800) 551-6712 Fax
www.gardens.com
info@gardeners.com

Gardens for Growing People
P.O. Box 630
Point Reyes, CA 94956
(415) 663-9433
(415) 663-9410 Fax
www.svn.net/growpepl
growpepl@svn.net

Let's Get Growing
1900 Commercial Way
Santa Cruz, CA 95065
(800) 408-1868
(831) 476-1427 Fax
www.letsgetgrowing.com
jhl@cruzio.com
Life Lab Science Program

National Audubon Society
700 Broadway
New York, NY 10003
(212) 979-3000
(212) 979-3188 Fax
www.audubon.org
webmaster@list.audubon.org

National Gardening Association
180 Flynn Avenue
Burlington, VT 05401
(802) 863-1308
(802) 863-5962 Fax
www2.garden.org/nga/

National Wildlife Federation
8925 Leesburg Pike
Vienna, VA 22184
(800) 822-9919
(703) 790-4000 Customer
   service
(703) 790-4040 Fax
www.nwf.org
info@nwf1.org
Backyard Habitat Program
www.nwf.org/habitats/

Rincon-Vitova Insectaries, Inc.
P.O. Box 1555
Ventura CA 93002
(800) 248-2847
(805) 643-5407 Customer
   service
(805) 643-6267 Fax
www.rinconvitova.com
bugnet@rinconvitova.com
Insectary

Wild Ones Natural
Landscapers, Inc.
P.O. Box 23576
Milwaukee, WI 53223-0576
(500) FOR-WILD (367-9453)
(920) 730-3986 Customer
   service
(920) 730-8654 Fax
www.for-wild.org

Xerces Society
4828 Southeast Hawthorne
   Boulevard
Portland, OR 97215-3252
(503) 232-6639
(503) 233-6794 Fax
www.xerces.org
xerces@teleport.com

Bibliography

Bailey, Liberty Hyde. *Cyclopedia of American Horticulture*. New York: Macmillan, 1900.

———. *The Garden of Gourds*. New York: Macmillan, 1900.

Bailey, Liberty Hyde, and Ethel Zoe. *Hortus Third*. New York: Macmillan, 1978.

Barash, Cathy Wilkinson. *Edible Flowers from Garden to Palate*. Golden, CO: Fulcrum, 1993.

———. *Evening Gardens*. Shelburne, VT: Chapters, 1993.

Barnhart, Robert K. *The American Heritage Dictionary of Science*. Boston: Houghton Mifflin, 1986.

Beckett, Kenneth. *Climbing Plants*. Portland, OR: Timber Press, 1983.

Buchmann, Stephen L. and Gary Paul Nabhan. *The Forgotten Pollinators*. Washington, DC, and Covelo, CA: Island Press/Shearwater Books, 1996.

Coombes, Allen J. *Dictionary of Plant Names*. Portland, OR: Timber Press, 1985.

Covell, Charles J. *Peterson Field Guide to Eastern Moths*. Boston: Houghton Mifflin, 1984.

De Bray, Lys. *Fantastic Garlands*. Poole, Dorset, England: Blandford Books, 1982.

———. *The Wild Garden*. New York: Mayflower Books, 1978.

Duke, James A., Ph.D. *Green Pharmacy*. Emmaus, PA: Rodale Press, 1997.

Earle, Alice Morse. *Child Life in Colonial Days*. New York: Macmillan, 1899.

———. *Old Time Gardens*. New York: Macmillan, 1901.

Freethy, Ron. *From Agar to Zenry*. Dover, NH: Tanager Books, 1985.

Friend, Hilderic. *Flowers and Flower Lore*. London: Swan, Sonnenschein, LeBas & Lowrey, 1886.

Garth, John and J.W. Tilden. *California Butterflies*. Berkeley: University of California Press, 1986.

Gibson, William Hamilton. *Eye Spy*. New York: Harper & Brothers, 1897.

———. *Sharp Eyes—A Rambler's Calendar*. New York: Harper & Brothers, 1891.

Griffiths, Mark. *The New Royal Horticultural Society Index of Garden Plants*. London: Macmillan Press, 1994.

Hogue, Charles L. *Insects of the Los Angeles Basin*. Los Angeles: Natural History Museum of Los Angeles County, 1993.

Keeley, Gertrude. *Story of the Wild Flowers for Young People*. New York: Hurst, 1914.

Loewer, Peter. *The Evening Garden*. New York: Macmillan, 1993.

Lovejoy, Sharon. *Hollyhock Days: Garden Adventures for the Young at Heart*. Loveland, CO: Interweave Press, 1994.

———. *Sunflower Houses: Garden Discoveries for Children of All Ages*. Loveland, CO: Interweave Press, 1991.

Martin, A., Herbert Zim, and Arnold Nelson. *American Wildlife and Plants: A Guide to Wildlife Food Habits.* New York: Dover Publications, 1951.

Martin, Laura L. *Garden Flower Folklore.* Chester, CT: Globe Pequot Press, 1987.

————. *Wildflower Folklore.* Charlotte, NC: Eat Wood Press, 1984.

Milne, Lorus, and Margery Milne. *National Audubon Society Field Guide to North America: Insects and Spiders.* New York: Alfred A. Knopf, 1980.

Morley, Margaret. *Butterflies and Bees: The Insect Folk.* Cambridge, MA: Ginn, 1905.

Newman, L. Hugh. *Create a Butterfly Garden.* London: John Baker, 1967.

O'Toole, Christopher, and Anthony Raw. *Bees of the World.* New York: Blandford, 1991.

Pellowski, Anne. *Hidden Stories in Plants.* New York: Macmillan, 1990.

Pyle, Robert M. *The Audubon Society Field Guide to North American Butterflies.* New York: Alfred A. Knopf, 1980.

Ransom, Jay Ellis. *Complete Field Guide to North American Wildlife.* New York: Harper & Row, 1981.

Editors of Smith & Hawken. *The Book of Outdoor Gardening.* New York: Workman, 1996.

Tekulsky, Mathew. *The Butterfly Garden.* Boston: Harvard Common Press, 1985.

Underhill, Ruth Murray. *Singing for Power.* Tucson: University of Arizona Press, 1938, reprinted 1993.

Wright, Amy Bartlett. *Peterson First Guide to Caterpillars.* Boston: Houghton Mifflin, 1993.

Xerces Society and Smithsonian Institution. *Butterfly Gardening: Creating Summer Magic in Your Garden.* San Francisco: Sierra Club Books, 1990.